MILLER'S

Treasure or Not?

HOW TO COMPARE & VALUE

AMERICAN
QUILTS

STELLA RUBIN

MILLER'S

Treasure or Not?

HOW TO COMPARE & VALUE

AMERICAN

QUILTS

STELLA RUBIN

This book is dedicated to my parents.

Miller's Treasure or Not?
How to Compare & Value
AMERICAN QUILTS

A Miller's–Mitchell Beazley book
Published by Octopus Publishing Group Ltd.
2-4 Heron Quays
London E14 4JP
UK

Mitchell Beazley Production Director: Julie Young
Mitchell Beazley Deputy Art Director: Vivienne Brar
Miller's Commissioning Editor: Anna Sanderson
Miller's Art Editor: Rhonda Fisher
Miller's U.S. Project Manager: Joseph Gonzalez

Produced by
Saraband, Inc.
9 Hunt Street
Rowayton, CT 06853
USA

Editor: Sara Hunt
Series Editor: Deborah DeFord
Volume Editor: Melanie Hulse, Deborah DeFord
Graphic Design: Dutton and Sherman
Editorial Assistants: Erin Pikor, Nikki L. Fesak
Proofreader & Indexer: Matt Levine

ISBN 1 84000 381 2

Set in Bembo 9.5/12
Produced by Toppan Printing Co., (HK) Ltd.
Printed and bound in China.

*On the cover: Star Pattern Charm Quilt, Lancaster, Pennsylvania, c.1880; back cover: detail from Mother-Daughter
Album Quilt, origin unknow, c.1855–1900.*

Contents

An Introduction to American Quilts

How to Use This Book

The unique compare-and-contrast format that is the hallmark of the *Miller's Treasure or Not?* series has been specially designed to help you to identify authentic American quilts and assess their value. At the heart of this book is a series of two-page comparison spreads—60 in all. On each spread, two quilts, related by type or pattern, are pictured on opposite pages and carefully analyzed to determine not only the market value of each quilt, but *why* one is more valuable than the other.

Throughout the comparison section, you'll be able to consider the context in which the pieces were created—both on the personal level of the quilt makers' lives and in the larger societal picture—their intended uses and relative condition, and their importance in today's quilt market. By comparing and analyzing a wide variety of quilts, you'll gain the knowledge and skills you'll need to find and evaluate American quilts on the market and assess their worth with confidence. The illustrations and call-outs, below and opposite, show how the various elements on a typical two-page comparison spread work.

The book's introductory chapters offer an overview of the quilt market and practical pointers on the care and display of your acquisitions. A fascinating history of quilting in America concludes with a magnificent picture gallery of top-of-the-line American quilts.

Finally, at the back of the book, you will find further information on where to see and buy American quilts, other sources of information that may advance your knowledge and understanding of the field, a glossary of quilting terminology, and a detailed index.

The *introduction* presents an overview of the quilt type or pattern, and its place in the quilt market today.

The *featured quilts* include one good example of the type or pattern quilt and one relatively better example.

The *call-outs* highlight each quilt's "value features"—key factors such as material, design, condition, and provenance that account for a quilt's relative market value.

The small *value boxes* (blue for the good piece, pink for the better piece) contain the size and potential value range of the featured quilt.

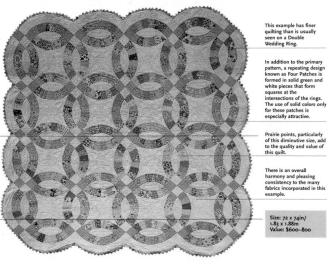

Double Wedding Ring

The quilt pattern most closely associated with the 1930s is the ever-popular Double Wedding Ring, which consists of interlocking circles. Each circle is made of squares of fabric, usually small-scale prints from dresses, aprons, or feed sacks. The printed fabrics are most often offset by complementary solid colors in the four squares forming the intersection of the circles.

Double Wedding Rings were sometimes made entirely of solid-color fabrics, but these are the exception. It is interesting to note that the Wedding Ring is one of the few patterns from the "outside world" used by Amish in the Midwest. The difference in this pattern when executed in the Amish palette of solid colors on a dark background is quite striking.

Double Wedding Ring quilts are almost always finished with scalloped edges. Rarely does the border extend beyond the outermost circles. Although scalloped edges make it more difficult for a collector to hang a quilt, this was not, of course, the purpose for which the piece was made: Scalloped edges fall gracefully over the sides of a bed.

While many collectors seek more unusual patterns, there is a steady market for the familiar patterns like the Double Wedding Ring. This pattern continued to be made into the 1950s, but the garish colors of the later examples make them less desirable for collectors.

Prairie-Point Edged Quilt, origin unknown, *c.* 1930

This example has finer quilting than is usually seen on a Double Wedding Ring.

In addition to the primary pattern, a repeating design known as Four Patches is formed in solid green and white pieces that form squares at the intersections of the rings. The use of solid colors only for these patches is especially attractive.

Prairie points, particularly of this diminutive size, add to the quality and value of this quilt.

There is an overall harmony and pleasing consistency to the many fabrics incorporated in this example.

Size: 72 x 74in/ 1.83 x 1.88m
Value: $600–800

154 Evaluating Quilts: By Pattern

The *headline* is a descriptive title for each featured quilt, followed by place of origin and an approximate date of creation.

Straight Border Edged Quilt, origin unknown, *c.* 1930

Many of the prints used in this example feature patterns with too large a scale for the size of the pieces they were selected for.

The pattern might have appeared more cohesive had there been greater consistency to the spacing of solid and printed fabrics.

This quilt is more easily hung for display than most Wedding Rings because it has a straight-edged border.

This example is nicely quilted, with four-lobed stylized flowers that fill the open white spaces.

Size: 77in/
1.96m square
Value: $300–600

The *captions* offer further specific information about a quilt's design and background.

▷ *This is a cotton quilt, c.1930, of unknown origin. The edging is finished with folded triangles, known as prairie points, and solid-color and printed fabrics are used consistently throughout.*

The *feature box* presents more information on a related type of quilt or quilt topic.

◁ *This is a cotton quilt, c.1930, of unknown origin. The edging is finished with folded triangles, known as prairie points, and solid-color and printed fabrics are used consistently throughout.*

Signed and Dated Quilts

The vast majority of collectible quilts were neither signed nor dated. In cases in which they were, the reference might or might not be to the maker and the time she completed her piece. The name could be that of the person for whom the quilt was created. The date could refer to an important event that occurred earlier, such as a birth or marriage.

In some instances, the choice of pattern may indicate a commemoration of a previous event. For instance, a Double Wedding Ring quilt, dated 1900, could not have been created in 1900 because the pattern did not exist until some thirty years

later. Familiarity with fabrics and quilting styles can also provide some valuable hints as to whether a date indicates when a quilt was made. Names are more difficult to determine. A male name is generally assumed to indicate the recipient, not the maker, although men were known to make quilts. Inscriptions appear in ink; embroidery; within the quilting; or, least often, in appliqué.

In rare cases, when a maker was especially proud of her work, she left no doubt as to who she was and how long she worked on her opus. For such a choice, the collector is grateful, because it provides invaluable

Cotton Quilt, Sunbonnet Sue Appliqué, Penn

Only Sue is appliquéd; all the other elements are embroidered.

Sue is wearing many feedsack prints, typical of the day.

It is rare to find an example in which she is engaged in a different activity in each block, with varied animals and flowers.

The embroidery is more detailed than usual, giving Sue fingers on her hands and shoes on her feet. (Usually Sue is an ambiguous female figure, with or without arms, but almost never with hands or feet.)

Size: 68 x 94in/
1.73 x 2.39m
Value: $800–1,200

◁ *This is the most standard format of Overall Sam. He is almost always an ambiguous figure, seen from the rear.*

▷ *This is an unusually lively interpretation of Sunbonnet Sue. It took a great deal of imagination, as well as skill, to design and embroider so many different motifs, all of which appear to have been done freehand.*

◁ *Appliqué and embroidery are combined in each block to give detail to the figure of Sue and the activity in which she is engaged.*

Sometimes, a feature box is replaced by a *detail* that offers a close-up view and further description of one of the example pieces.

Understanding the Market

When I was a fledgling quilt buyer, an old-timer offered me the following advice—buy the best you can afford. In time, I learned that he was right. The best quilts are the ones that appreciate most in value over time. They are also the ones most likely to hold your interest for as long as you own them. Inexpensive pieces, usually the more common and easy to find, tend to lose their appeal, and as your experience and taste evolve, their commonness becomes more apparent.

Stretching your dollar limit at the outset will work to your advantage in the long run: you will have a quilt you can continue to enjoy, and when it's time to sell, you will likely get a better price. Not all pieces that cost a lot are worth a lot, however. How do you determine value?

How do you distinguish between a great quilt, a good one, and one that is only so-so?

Rule number one: know what's out there. Familiarize yourself with the range of possibilities. Look at books. The more patterns, styles, and colors to which you expose yourself, the better able you will be to "place" a particular quilt in the overall market.

Go to museums. There, you'll find worthy examples that have been researched and documented. You'll begin not only to have a sense of how to identify an authentic antique but also how to judge its condition in comparison to others of like vintage. Visiting shops, antique shows, and auctions will increase your knowledge along these lines, as well.

▶ *This is just a small section of a Competitive quilt dating from c.1880. The side of each triangle measures just ³⁄₈ in/0.95cm. The fact that the piecing was done with such precision, along with the unique approach of replacing some triangles with printed fabric faces, gives this quilt exceptional value ($10,000+).*

Nothing substitutes, obviously, for the tactile experience of handling a quilt. Only by touch can you tell such things as whether a quilt is limp from multiple washings or firm because it has never been washed and still retains the sizing in the fabric. Quilts in the latter group—those in an unused, unwashed condition—tend to be more desirable, despite the potential occurrence of small spots or irregularities in color. There is no consensus, and no right or wrong answer, on the question of whether a quilt should be washed or not. It depends on individual preference. Some people want a quilt with the never-washed feel; others want to know that a quilt does not have a century of surface dirt on it before they use it on a bed.

Hands-on examination also reveals details about stitching, fabrics, and color that photographs cannot completely convey. Handling the quilt allows you to gauge the weight and thickness of the layers and to better examine the relation of front to back, and binding to block. Quilts, by their nature, are intended to be touched and used, and the fuller your experience of a particular quilt, the better equipped you'll be to judge its appeal and worth.

Exposure to as many different quilts as possible is key to understanding the market. Only by familiarizing yourself with what is ordinary and easy to find do you learn what is rare. And only by gaining knowledge about the making, styling, and uses of quilts can you appreciate the value factors that make some quilts more desirable than others.

Knowing the Value Factors

Technique is one of the aspects by which a quilt is judged, but it is important to understand how a quilt maker's technique may or may not actually affect value. For example, many people feel that appliqué quilts, by

◄ These close-ups come from two Basket quilts. While both quilts use the basket shape, the lower example is far less complex in construction. Ordinarily, this would detract from the value. However, in the case of the two Basket quilts shown here, the overall pattern of the lower quilt is more imaginative and thus more valuable.

definition, are better than pieced quilts. While it is true that appliqués were more often made as "best" quilts, not all of them were successful. By the same token, most utilitarian quilts were made by piecing, but not all pieced quilts were utilitarian. The range of possibilities for both methods is infinite. Lancaster County Amish quilts, for instance, are among the most highly valued. Yet they were not only made by piecing, they were made with very large pieces. The latter aspect of pieced quilts usually detracts from their value. The more you learn about how these factors interplay in the world of antique quilts, the more you will be able to evaluate each quilt on its own merits.

Another value point for quilts is their patterns. A quilt design is usually judged by its complexity, harmony, and general success as a pattern. There are some designs that are by their nature complex. Others have simple concepts but can be rendered with a great deal of detail and skill. Quilt makers may choose colors or variations on a basic design that create something exeptional from it, sometimes building from a single design to create one or more secondary patterns.

Because rarity is another of the important criteria in determining value, it's important that you weigh the success of the pattern against its availability in the market. The first time you see a Double Wedding Ring, you may find the pattern fascinating. By the time you've seen several dozen, you will come to realize that a great many Double Wedding Rings appeared in the 1930s, particularly compared to other patterns. In other words, you may want to wait for a quilt that appears less frequently.

Rarity has a tremendous effect on the market value of a quilt. In a quilt of extraordinary rarity, more flaws in condition are acceptable than in a more common pattern. Sufficient numbers of everyday quilts still exist so that you do not have to buy one in poor condition—an old quilt need not be an abused one. Often sellers describe a quilt as "in good condition for its age." Experience has taught me that I probably will not buy such a quilt. A surprising number of old quilts were packed away and never used or brought out only for special occasions. These are the ones I want to buy.

▶ *A close view of this Mariner's Compass quilt shows the remarkable precision with which the quilt maker rendered curved forms and fine tips—among the most difficult to accomplish. Such workmanship is part of the reason that the quilt is valued at $8,000 and up.*

But superior technique, unusual interpretation of pattern, and even rarity do not count for much if you do not like a particular quilt. This brings me to the second critical rule of thumb: buy what you love. Buy what gives you a visceral reaction. Buy what makes your heart race. Ask yourself, "If I leave this and come back to find that it's already sold, how will I feel?"

As both a buyer and seller, I am familiar with the agony of "passer's remorse." Real regret over the very appealing quilts I failed to acquire occurs far more frequently than the chagrin over the ones I did buy and later regretted. I have seen many people spend years trying to find a substitute for the quilt that got away. What stopped them from buying it when they could? Often it was simply a lack of confidence in their own reaction to a lovely piece of work. Don't call in a committee of your friends and family in the hopes of reaching consensus. If you are the one who is going to live with a quilt, buy what you want, not what someone else tells you to want. The more opinions you solicit, the more confused you are likely to become. Trust yourself.

Knowing the Market

Collecting quilts does not need to be financially intimidating. Prices range widely, allowing collectors of all stripes to buy at levels comfortable to them. Interesting examples can easily be found for hundreds of dollars, although the range can extend into the hundreds of thousands. By far, the greatest number of quilts on the market today can be purchased for less than $5,000; only a handful have brought more than $100,000.

Several factors are involved in the relative affordability of quilts. For one thing, women's work has historically been undervalued and underappreciated. In addition, the makers of most quilts remain anonymous—we do not know who they were and we can only guess at what they intended. Some arbiters of the art world are reluctant to attribute the full status and price of fine art to an anonymous genre. In the last 10 or more years, the price range of needlework samplers has far outstripped that of quilts, due, for the most part, to the availability of historical

◀ *One of the ways in which a quilt's value is increased is through the creative use of multiple patterns. In this detail of a Bear's Paw quilt, one can pick out a square surrounded by diamonds, a series of arrows that point out toward the corners from center, and of course, the Bear's Paw.*

and genealogical information on the sampler makers. However, the critics' lack of appreciation for the intrinsic merits of the quilt, regardless of who made it, is the collector's gain. For those who can enjoy the colors, pattern, fabric, design, and needlework of a quilt without knowing the details of its origin, the quilt market offers excellent value. It is interesting to note that for the relatively few quilts for which we have such background information—a nice feature, to be sure—the price does not rise astronomically.

In spite of many years buying and selling quilts, I still find pricing one of the most difficult aspects of the business. Despite some guidelines as to which basic patterns sell for how much, pricing is subject to variation among sellers. This may owe to the seller's available supply, or it may depend on regional preferences and expectations of cost. The issue of price becomes even

more difficult in the case of rare or unique examples. Inevitably, subjectivity plays a part with buyer and seller alike. In large part, I base selling prices on the original cost of a piece to me. Nevertheless, my personal aesthetic reaction to the quilt cannot help but enter into my thinking, as well. The reaction of a possible buyer plays its part in what that person may be willing to pay.

In terms of finding good deals, do not assume that a trip to the hinterlands will yield a treasure-trove of inexpensive quilts. Those days are over. Many of the best quilts have long since been culled by established quilt sellers, and what remains tends to be the detritus. Neither assume that you will pay exorbitant prices by buying from established sellers, nor that you will find comparable pieces for a fraction in the country. In some rural areas, you may actually find higher prices than in the cities. Trends and fashions exist in the quilt market as they do

▶ *A quilt maker may enhance the ultimate value of a quilt by the decision to take a traditional pattern and render it in a more elaborate way. In this Alphabet quilt detail, the images were appliquéd rather than embroidered in the usual manner, producing a stronger overall effect.*

in any other field. The best value can usually be found in what is not the hottest style or pattern at the moment. If you acquire a quality piece that is currently out of fashion, you will usually see the cycle return to favor that type, and you will, in the meantime, have made a good deal for a very favorable price. By educating yourself, you will be able to make the best purchases, regardless of where you are, geographically and in the trend cycle.

Having said all that I have about factors in the quilt market, I continue to maintain that the best guideline for successful buying is to focus on what give you the most positive reaction, whether it is based on color, pattern, stitching, rarity, or a combination of the above. By familiarizing yourself with many types of quilts, you will train your judgment and learn to trust it. One of the wonderful aspects of collecting is that you make your own rules. Some people buy quilts made in a particular period or limit the patterns they buy. Others choose specific colors. Still others prefer eclectic collections that offer them a range of styles, patterns, or periods. It is not a question of right choices and wrong ones; the market leaves room for every knowledgeable collector to be right.

After nearly 30 years of buying and selling quilts, I have now become the old-timer echoing the advice of my elder—buy the best you can afford. It is most likely to hold your interest and increase in value. Educate yourself. Find out what is on the market. Learn what kinds of quilts were made and what you find most engaging. Once you have done that, trust yourself. Buy what you love. Collecting is an act of passion: it is not the place for pure rationality. I have offered guidelines, but they are just that. They are not hard and fast rules, for there are none. Go out there, and enjoy the hunt.

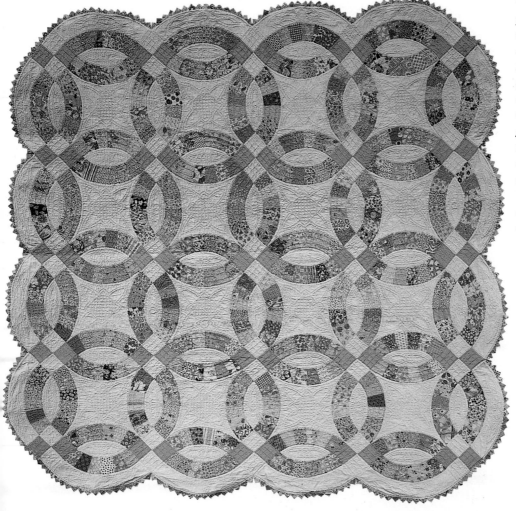

◀ *Even the most common patterns become uncommon when given extraordinary details. This Double Wedding Ring quilt has exceptional quilting and Prairie Point edging. Both choices raise the value of the quilt. The quilt's greatest virtue in the eyes of the collector, however, may simply be that he or she finds it personally appealing. That's quite enough to make a piece valuable to the one who purchases it.*

Caring for Quilts

The question most frequently asked of an antique quilt dealer is this: "How can I wash my quilt?" The wise advisor offers no single answer. Each quilt must be considered on the basis of age, fabrics, and general condition. In some instances, washing a quilt can do more harm than good. The quilt owner must maintain a fine balance between the risks of washing an antique quilt versus allowing stains to remain that may do continuing damage to the fabrics. Washing is not out of the question, but neither is it necessarily the only or best choice.

Under no circumstances should dry cleaning be considered for cotton or linen quilts. The process will usually not remove stains on these fabrics, and chemical residue may cause further long term damage. With silk, velvet, or wool quilts, on the other hand, dry cleaning may be the only cleaning choice.

Often, a quilt can be sufficiently freshened by airing it for a day. Ideally, this is done outdoors, away from direct sunlight. For several reasons, it is advisable to do this at least once a year. First, it offers the opportunity to examine a quilt for damage. Second, it necessitates refolding the quilt for storage. Creases can become permanent if the quilt is folded in the same way for long periods. Not least of all, airing a quilt that is usually stored presents an opportunity to enjoy it.

Surface dirt can be removed by gently vacuuming over the quilt. The nozzle should be placed several inches above the quilt; it should not be used directly on it. For greater protection, a fine, clean, mesh screening can be placed over the entire quilt. Vacuuming is the safest method for cleaning quilts with glazed fabrics or with materials that are not colorfast.

The demands of washing an antique quilt defy generalization. Many people do wash their own quilts, but they face inherent risks in doing so. Dyes were not always as stable as those to which we are accustomed today. In addition, it may be close to impossible to determine the conditions to which the quilt has been subjected and how they will affect wet cleaning. The earlier the vintage of the quilt, the more unknowns exist. When done without sufficient care and knowledge, wet cleaning can cause tremendous damage. If your quilt is of great sentimental and/or monetary value, you may be better served to err on the side of caution. Consult a local museum to locate a professional conservator who has the facilities and expertise to do the job properly.

Should you decide to wash your quilt, you will first need to test each fabric in it for colorfastness. Use water from an eyedropper to wet the fabric. Blot it with a soft white cloth. Only if no color shows on the blotting cloth

▶ *This Victorian Crazy quilt, c.1884, is made from velvet and satin fabrics. A quilt of such material and vintage is a definite candidate for the attentions of a professional conservator.*

is it safe to proceed with wet cleaning. Use a gentle washing solution in warm water.

Machine washing is not recommended. Ideally, you should wash a quilt in a vat large enough so that the piece can be laid out flat—this usually means washing the quilt in a bathtub. Even so, you'll probably have to fold the quilt, which makes it cumbersome to rinse. It is not uncommon to have to rinse it as many as half a dozen times to remove all of the soap. Removing the quilt from the tub requires support beneath it. The weight of the water makes the quilt very heavy, and the fabrics may incur damage if not properly supported. For the same reason, experts advise against hanging the quilt on a line to dry. It should be laid out flat and blotted above and below with clean cloth towels. Fans can be helpful in drying the quilt more quickly. Never place an antique quilt in a dryer.

Light is one of the greatest enemies of textiles. It can cause the fibers to break down and fade—both irreversible forms of damage. Natural ultraviolet light is the most damaging, but even long periods of artificial light, particularly fluorescent, can do harm. For maximum protection, quilts, like all textiles, need to be kept in moderate temperatures and humidity. Avoid storing them in the basement or the attic. Too much humidity can cause the growth of mold and mildew. Silverfish and other insects thrive in damp areas. Too hot or dry an environment can cause fabrics to become overdry and brittle.

Quilts should also be stored with as few folds as possible. One of the best ways to avoid unnecessary folding is to roll the quilt around a cardboard tube that is at least 3 inches in diameter and several inches longer than the quilt. The tube should be covered with acid-free tissue paper or a well-washed sheet of cotton or muslin upon which the quilt is then rolled with the top facing inward. This minimizes the strain on the stitching.

If the quilt must be stored folded on a shelf, in a blanket chest, or in a cardboard box, take care that the fabric does not touch the wood or paper. These materials contain acids that can stain the quilt. Again, several layers of acid-free tissue paper or a washed sheet of cotton or muslin provides excellent protection. Sharp creases are best avoided by crumpling acid-free tissue inside the folds to round them out. Do not stack many quilts on top of each other, for their weight can also create sharp creases. Commercially available acid-free boxes easily provide separate storage for each quilt.

A spare bed is one of the best places to store an antique quilt. Place it fully open on the bed, either pattern-side down or up, and cover it with a sheet to avoid exposure to light. The mattress provides even support and makes it unnecessary to fold the fabric.

Sealed plastic bags are to be avoided at all costs. They prevent fabrics from breathing and can trap harmful moisture. While moth balls are helpful in preventing insect damage to a wool quilt in a sealed blanket chest, care must be taken to make sure that the mothballs do not come in direct contact with the fabric.

In sum, the greatest enemies of quilts are light, extremes of temperature and humidity, and bugs. All can be avoided with minimal care and cost to lengthen the life of your antique quilt.

◀ *This cotton Schoolhouse quilt, c.1890, has almost certainly lost quite a lot of its original color through light exposure and/or laundering. What now looks tan probably began as dark green.*

Displaying Quilts

Most quilts were made as functional objects. Many have survived more than 150 years and will continue to last if handled with a modicum of care and respect. When choosing a quilt, consider the use to which you plan to put it. Some are obviously much more durable than others. If you are planning to use your quilt on a child's bed, for instance, it might be best to select one from the early 20th century that is likely to withstand more washing and use than an earlier example. A quilt on a guest-room bed or hung on a wall will be handled less and could make you comfortable with an earlier and perhaps more fragile piece.

When using your quilt on a bed, be sure to use a sheet underneath it. This will minimize the effects of body oils on the fabrics. For the same reason, it is best, when the pattern allows for it, to rotate the direction of the quilt on the bed. The end toward the head inevitably gets the most

wear from being tugged and pulled and has the most contact with the oils in your hands. Try not to share your bed with your pets when the quilt is on. Cats and dogs can do terrible damage to antique fabrics. Use care when tucking the quilt under the mattress, particularly on an old bed. Bedsprings have ruined many fine quilts.

A quilt also makes a wonderful decorative accent when used as a throw over a table or sofa. It can provide a splash of color and design even when not viewed entirely. Nothing provides a cozier cover when you are sitting on the sofa and need just a little bit of warmth. The wonderful tactile quality of a soft quilt, combined with beautiful fabrics, pattern, and color, is hard to surpass, regardless of how the quilt is being used.

Consider, as well, where you are going to use the quilt. Whether displaying your quilt on a bed or a wall, care must be taken that it receives minimal exposure to

Display Do's & Don'ts

• *Many people choose to hang a quilt by sewing a sleeve to the back and placing a wall-mounted rod through the sleeve. The fabric used for the sleeve should be cotton or muslin that has been washed to remove any chemicals or sizing. The dowel or bracket should never come in direct contact with the quilt.*

• *Another popular method for hanging a quilt uses Velcro™. A strip of Velcro™ is sewn along at least one length of the quilt. The corresponding half of the strip is stapled to a wood strip that is nailed to the wall. You only need to use the Velcro™ across the top edge of the quilt to assure equal weight distribution, but some*

people prefer to make a wood frame and attach the quilt on all four sides. This has the aesthetic advantage of giving the quilt the look of a painting stretched on a canvas. From the point of view of preservation, either method is suitable.

• *Another variation is to sew Velcro™ on all four sides (if the pattern of the quilt allows it to be hung from all sides), even though the quilt will be attached only at the top. This allows for convenient rotation of the side from which the quilt is hung. This is desirable for the sake of the quilt's life. Hanging the quilt creates a certain amount of unavoidable stress on the fabrics that can be offset by the rotation.*

• *Staples, nails, clips, pins, and tabs that penetrate or touch the fabric of the quilt are to be avoided, as they place strain on particular areas and may mark the fabric or damage fibers. In a short time, they lead to distortion of the quilt's shape.*

• *Glass or plexiglass box frames are useful for keeping dust away from your quilt. It is essential, though, that spacers be placed in the case to prevent the glass and the fabric from touching. That contact encourages the growth of mold and mildew. Allow for air circulation by using cotton across the back of the frame.*

• *If you display your quilt over a banister or rod, be sure*

that the wood is sealed. For added protection, place a cotton sheet between the wood and the quilt.

• *If you own more than one quilt, it is best to rotate which quilts are displayed every few months to give each one a "rest." Ideally, a quilt should not be kept on continuous display.*

• *The preceding warnings are not meant to discourage buyers from using and enjoying their quilts. They are simply a reminder that quilts that have lasted through the decades were made with love and great care many years ago. They should be carefully and lovingly used, displayed, and appreciated today.*

light. Both natural and artificial light do irreversible damage to textiles. The less light the better. Ultraviolet (UV) filtering materials are available that are of some benefit in minimizing the effects of natural light. Keeping the shades or curtains drawn as much as possible is a wise precaution.

Fireplaces and wood stoves, on the other hand, do not constitute a light hazard but give off barely perceptible amounts of smoke that build up over time and cause quilts to yellow. Cooking oils also take a long-term toll by depositing a film on fabrics.

Many quilt owners feel most comfortable displaying antique quilts as wall hangings. Several methods work well for hanging a quilt. Regardless of the particular method, what is most important is that the weight of the quilt be evenly distributed. Once that is assured, the specific method used is a matter of individual taste.

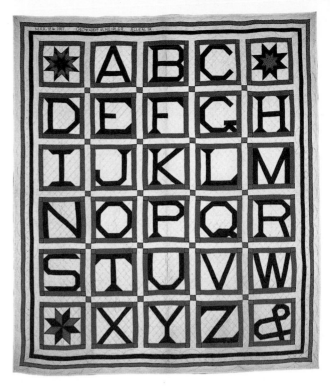

Alphabet cotton quilt, Pennsylvania, c.1917.

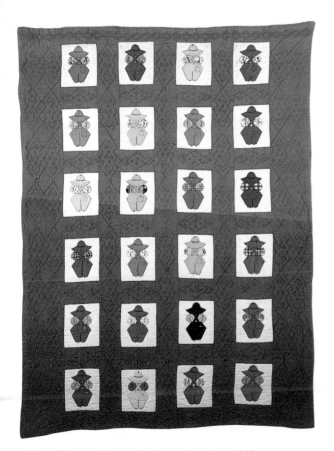

Overall Sam cotton quilt, Pennsylvania, c.1930.

◄▲ *While the wisdom of using either of these antiques as a child's bedcover might be questioned, there is no doubt that the Overall Sam quilt is the better choice from a preservationist's point of view. While this Sam is a relatively simple version of its pattern and valued at approximately $400–$800 on the quilt market today, the older Alphabet quilt is an exceptional example of its style. It is in pristine, unwashed condition and could easily bring $10,000 or more on the open market. It deserves museum-caliber care.*

An American Quilts Primer

A common belief persists that quilting is an art that developed in colonial America. While early American colonists certainly took the form and created a seemingly infinite number of pattern variations within it, the art of quilting actually began long before their arrival in North America, and it developed in geographical locations far from North American shores.

The earliest known examples of quilting are garments rather than bed coverings. One such example—quilted garb on a carved ivory figure—dates to 3400 BC. Quilted fabric for floor coverings and clothing was found in the tombs of Egyptian pharaohs between the 1st century BC and the 2nd century AD. The application of quilting to clothing continued through the centuries, and was used between the 11th and 13th centuries to create protective garments to be worn both under and over metal armor.

The earliest known bed quilt is a Sicilian piece, made at the end of the 14th century. This is a Pictorial quilt *(see page 86)* that depicts scenes from the romantic legend of Tristan and Isolde. The extraordinary quilted detail in this piece strongly suggests that by the time it was constructed, the tradition of quilted bedcovers had been underway for quite a while. During the 15th century, a thriving cottage industry developed in Marseilles, France, for the making of quilted clothing and bedcovers. At the same time, commercially produced quilted covers arrived in Europe as imports from India. Such widespread use of quilted material is hardly surprising. Quilted bedcovers, clothing, and curtains provide a perennially practical solution to the need for insulation and warmth, and in many cases, a highly practical way to recycle fabrics.

The earliest surviving American quilts date to the 18th century. Typically designed in a center-medallion format *(see pages 40–43)*, they displayed a pattern that consisted of a single, central motif surrounded by multiple borders. The motif was either quilted, pieced, or appliquéd. But beginning in the 1830s, the prevailing style began to shift. Pieced blocks, and by the 1850s— when virtually all domestically made fabric was

▶ *Pieced Center Medallion quilt, Virginia, c.1790. This is a fine example of those few quilts that survive from the 18th century.*

commercially manufactured—the repeat block format with which we are most familiar today, had become the dominant styles.

By the mid-19th century, quilt making had entered its heyday. Fabric was more affordable and available. Women had more leisure time to devote to needlework and few other sanctioned avenues for creative expression. The role of fine artist was not considered ladylike because it distracted a woman from homemaking. This cult of domesticity prevailed through the 1860s. Thus, the needle arts and quilting, in particular, became the means by which women could express their creativity while at the same time maintaining the home.

What is a Quilt?

Whether antique or modern, most quilts consist of three layers: a top, an interlining known as batting, and a backing. The top contains the design. In antique quilts, the batting was usually cotton. Wool was also a common choice, but almost anything could be used. Some quilt makers inserted quilts that were in very poor condition into newer quilts; others used blankets. From time to time, quilts were made with no batting—just a top and a backing. Most often, these were summer spreads. Some, however, were made without batting to allow the quilter the flexibility to create extraordinarily fine designs—designs that would be impossible if the quilt included a bulky batting. The third layer, the backing, was often one of the fabrics used on the quilt top, but any fabric would serve. Some quilters chose backings made of a loosely woven fabric that would allow a special quilting technique, called trapunto *(see page 145)*, that involved adding extra batting in places to accentuate the quilting. In the second half of the 19th century, a commercially made fabric known as cheater's cloth became a popular choice for backing quilts. Cheater's cloth *(see page 141)* was cotton printed with designs that mimicked patchwork patterns.

The layers of the quilt are held together with ties or, more commonly, stitching. In their most basic form, the ties or stitching serve a purely functional purpose; they hold the quilt layers together and keep the batting from shifting during use or washing. Many tied quilts were made of heavy wool. In these, the layers were held

◄ *Cheater's cloth. Notice that the fabric is designed to look as though it were pieced patchwork. The blue/green palette shown here is unusual.*

together by yarn, thread, or ribbon that was looped through the layers at intervals of approximately 6in/15cm and knotted. This was far less time- and labor-intensive than quilting and still resulted in a serviceable bedcover. As the artistic elements of quilt making gained dominance over the utilitarian, the stitching—also known as quilting—became a primary means of decoration. The quilting became a separate element of the design that not only showcased the quilt maker's skill but also expressed her creative vision. In some instances, the quilting provided the sole decoration, as in Whitework and Wholecloth quilts *(see pages 44–47).*

The Origins of American Quilts

Immigrants to the New World brought their Old World needlecraft traditions with them. As settlements evolved into colonies and colonies grew to become states, the shifting populations borrowed from one another's traditions and created the many pattern variations that have kept the love of quilts and quilting alive into the present.

In the earliest days of settlement, fabric was difficult to make and extremely expensive to import. Its scarcity made it precious, and its use was carefully husbanded. Articles of clothing might be worn for 20 years or more, then cut down for a child or refashioned into household linens such as towels or curtains. Worn wool clothing was painstakingly unraveled and the yarn reused for socks or mittens. Only when all other uses had been exhausted would material be relegated to the scrap bag for use in a quilt. This meant that quilts were made from fabrics that might already have seen some 50 years of use. It is no wonder, then, that no American quilts made prior to the 18th century have survived.

But while most people could scarcely afford fabric in any quantity, for the wealthy, cost was hardly an issue. The colonial upper classes favored two types of refined quilts that were either imported from Europe and India or made in America by professional quilt makers: Wholecloth quilts made of elegant silks or wools *(see page 46)* and exquisite bedcovers made of chintz in an appliqué technique called broderie perse. Although several existing examples of both types can be documented to the early 18th century, quilts were not common household items at this time. The few that did exist were valued more highly than other types of bed coverings, such as blankets and bed rugs.

▶ *Tree of Life, Philadelphia, Penn.,* c.*1800. The quilt maker used the broderie perse technique of appliqué to create this design.*

Quilt Types and Patterns

There are three methods by which quilt tops are decorated: quilting alone, piecing, and appliqué. Every quilt has some form of stitching; many examples combine appliqué and piecing. In piecing, which is also known as patchwork, shapes—usually geometric shapes such as squares, triangles, and circles or portions of circles—are cut from different fabrics and sewn together, essentially creating a new fabric. Many everyday quilts were made by piecing, but extraordinary quilts also resulted from the technique. Some examples are composed of thousands of tiny pieces that refract into multiple patterns. Surely the makers of these intended as fine bedcovers as those working with appliqué, which many collectors consider the more elegant style.

Most of the quilts made as "best" quilts were done by appliqué. (A best quilt is one that was made more for decoration than for use as a bedcover.) But there is a range of elegance in appliqué just as there is in patchwork, with the Sunbonnet Sue pattern *(see page 160)* falling in the homier range and Tree of Life examples *(see page 98)* being among the most refined. Appliqué involves cutting shapes or printed images (such as flowers or butterflies) from one fabric and sewing them on another. Appliqué was especially popular in the United States in the mid-19th century, and countless examples, frequently in combinations of red and green fabrics, were made.

From these techniques, an astonishing variety of types and patterns arose. Quilt types are broad categories of design choices, irrespective of pattern. They may reflect a format choice, such as Center Medallion, Wholecloth, or Strip quilts. They may come from a community's shared aesthetic, such as Lancaster County and Midwest Amish quilts or Baltimore Album quilts. Or they may be made for a specific purpose, as are Friendship and Fundraising quilts. Patterns are simply standardized designs.

Quilt patterns were not widely published until late in the 19th century. Before that, patterns were more idiosyncratic, and quilts made earlier in the century seem as varied as the women who made them. Patterns were handed down from mother to daughter and within families. Women exchanged patterns among themselves and saw the work of others at agricultural fairs. This resulted in similarities among the patterns used within communities but a tremendous amount of latitude in how each one was interpreted. Once patterns began to be published in magazines and other periodicals, this trend continued on a national scale. In large part, regional and individual differences became homogenized, and the originality that formerly went into creating patterns was channeled into interpreting them.

A Chronicle in Fabric

Quilts quite literally offer a history of the United States. The names given to patterns and the images within them often reflect the social and political concerns and issues of the times in which they were made. Quilts made with patterns called Rocky Road to Kansas, Arkansas Traveler, and Delectable Mountains *(see page 112)* were popular as the United States was pushing westward. Bear's Paw *(see page 134)*, Wild Goose Chase *(see page 102)*, and Log Cabin *(see pages 108–111)* indicated the concerns of women on the frontier, while Ocean Waves *(see page 126)* and Mariner's Compass *(see page 118)* evoked the cares of those women who lived on the coasts.

Vocations were celebrated in names such as Carpenter's Square, Carpenter's Wheel, and Mill Wheel, and spiritual traditions were commemorated in patterns such as Star of Bethlehem and Joseph's Coat *(see page 140)*. Political issues and social concerns were noted in the patterns Lincoln's Platform, Whig Rose *(see page 144)*, and Whig's Defeat. New York was not the only state to be honored with a pattern *(see New York Beauty, page 116)*; nearly every state has its name incorporated in at least one quilt pattern. Personal concerns, as well, were noted, and patterns were dubbed Old Maid's Ramble, Bachelor's Puzzle, and Lover's Knot.

The production of these patterns did not occur in a single era, but their names continue to acknowledge the relevant issues and concerns that originally inspired them. Pattern names reveals a great deal about both the interests of the burgeoning nation and the lives of the women who made quilts. Quilts also reveal a great deal about the fashions of the times. Victorian Crazy quilts, for example, feature the highly elaborate fabrics and patterns popular in most decorative arts of that era.

Quilts were made to celebrate all of life's major milestones. In effect, women autobiographies were designed into their quilts. A Crib quilt greeted a new child *(see page 72)*. A young girl learned valuable skills by making a Doll quilt *(see page 74)*. A Freedom quilt commemorated a young man's reaching the age of majority or completing an apprenticeship. Wedding quilts celebrated marriage. Album, Friendship, and Signature quilts usually marked the departure of an important member of the community *(see pages 50–55)*. Mourning or Widow's quilts memorialized the dear departed. All of the important themes of a woman's life were expressed in the making of quilts.

On a broader scale, quilts also offered a significant means of expressing feelings about social and political events. During the Civil War, supporters of the abolitionist movement made quilts to express their views. Women of both the North and South made countless numbers of quilts as fundraisers for military and medical supplies *(see page 68)*. Each time a state was admitted to the Union, women announced their allegiance through the quilts they made. The Women's Christian Temperance Union sought support of their views with the numerous Fundraising quilts they made *(see page 128)*. In times of war, Patriotic quilts abounded *(see page 66)*.

Bees and Frolics

Before the Industrial Revolution, needlework was one of the first and most important skills that young girls learned. It was not uncommon to begin at the age of 2 or 3. In some households, a girl was expected to complete a quilt by her fifth birthday—and to have a dozen in her hope chest by the time she married. Not all females learned to read and write, but like it or not, they all learned to sew.

Although many of the finest quilt examples probably come from the work of a single person, the enormous labor involved in making a quilt was not always a solo undertaking. Women quilted with family members at home or at events known as quiltings, quilt frolics, or quilting bees. At a bee, women gathered to quilt the tops that had already been appliquéd or pieced. Everyone could find a place at the event. Those most skilled with

needles did most of the sewing. Women who were less adept with needles prepared the food; young girls threaded needles and learned from the adults.

In addition to lightening the burden by sharing the labor, quilting bees fostered a sense of community for women. In frontier and rural areas, where settlements might be widely scattered, getting together to quilt provided a rich and rare opportunity for socializing. Women exchanged recipes, quilt patterns, fabric, political views, community news, and gossip. (In one diary account, a woman stated that she *had* to attend quiltings, because if she did not, she might be the one they were talking about.)

Quilting bees lost some of their festive aspect in the mid-19th century. Women no longer gathered to make quilts simply for themselves and their neighbors, but rather for the needy at home and abroad under the somber aegis of the church. But as always, the bees continued to afford women the opportunity to exchange ideas and opinions, not only on domestic concerns, but also on politics and issues. Susan B. Anthony made her first speech advocating women's suffrage at a quilting bee.

Material Concerns

Prior to 1820, virtually all domestically made fabric in the United States was homespun, and making this cloth

▶ *Susan B. Anthony quilt, origin unknown, c.1912. Anthony helped lead the Women's Suffrage movement in the early 20th century. This patriotic quilt was no doubt created to raise funds for the suffrage cause.*

was a long and laborious process. A year and a half could pass from the time flax seed was planted to the time the plants were harvested and the fibers spun to make linen thread—which then had to be woven into cloth. Shearing, carding, spinning, and weaving wool took only slightly less time. In addition to making their own thread and fabric, women also created their own dyes, primarily from plants that also had to be cultivated.

After 1820, commercially manufactured fabric was readily available from American mills and cost a fraction of what had previously been imported. Women from a wide range of economic classes could afford to purchase lengths of new fabric specifically for almost any use. Quilt making was freed from the constraints of a salvage art.

The Art and Craft of Quilts

When looking at a quilt as a work of art, as a painting in fabric, it can be helpful to apply criteria similar to those used to evaluate paintings. You needn't analyze every element in order to enjoy a particular quilt, but being aware of the criteria will give you a greater appreciation for the quilter's art. You will better understand why some quilts are more successful than others. The criteria are originality, composition (pattern and design), color and texture, proportion and form, and craftsmanship.

Originality is one of the most important criteria in evaluating any work of art, and quilts are no exception. Many of the most successful examples are those in which the quilt makers created unique variations of known patterns or combined fabrics imaginatively to create novel secondary patterns or dimensions. These quilts convey a spontaneity and individuality that is not evident in conventional renderings of established patterns, regardless of how skillfully they may be constructed.

The first question to ask is whether the pattern creates a unified whole. Ideally, the composition is equally interesting throughout the quilt. Is it balanced and harmonious? Is the design cohesive? Does it have rhythmic movement that leads your eye throughout the pattern or do you get bogged down in one area? Are some areas too weak or too strong, diminishing the unity of the piece? Second, the pattern should appear to be contained within the whole. Many quilts that do not have borders look as though they were artificially cut short; the pattern seems to run off the edges. When there is a border treatment, does it relate well to the entire composition of the quilt? Does it enhance the main pattern?

Some collectors feel that the more complex the pattern, the better. This is one measure of success, but not necessarily a decisive one. The quilts made by the Amish in Lancaster County *(see pages 76–79)*, for example, use patterns that have only a few, very large pieces. They are

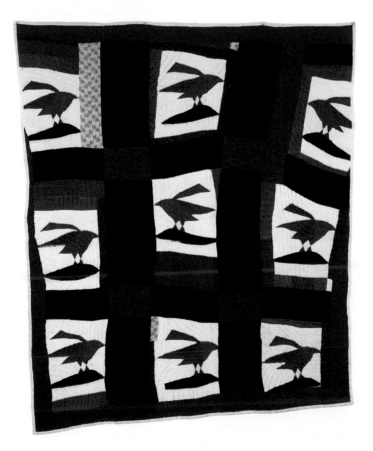

◀ *African-American quilt, made by Blanche Ransome Parker, Supervisor of Black Schools in Carroll County, Tenn.,*c.*1940. While Parker's needlework might not garner awards, her use of color, pattern, and original design make this an exceptional piece.*

minimal and pared down to the extreme, yet they are among the most universally appreciated—and highly valued—quilts in the market, largely because of their simplicity and their exquisite use of color.

Color and texture are two of a quilt's most important features. If the fabrics are unpleasant to the touch, they detract from the quilt's overall value. Quilters often combine different materials, such as wool, silk, and velvet, or different weights and weaves of the same fabric, usually cotton, in one quilt. Do the textures harmonize well? Do the fabrics feel good to the touch? Does the texture created by the quilting make it more inviting? Ask yourself whether the colors and textures work well together. Quilts also often combine an array of fabrics with many prints and colors. Are they compatible? Do they satisfy the eye? Are the scales of the prints in pleasing proportions?

Next, consider the overall proportion and form of the quilt's components. How do the various elements relate to one another in terms of their size and shape? Is the scale proportional? Is there interesting interplay between light and dark colors? Are the shapes pleasing and engaging? They need to be pleasing, but not necessarily realistic. For example, a tiny urn might hold a huge bouquet of flowers that, in real life, would topple over. On a quilt, the stylization can be charming.

Craftsmanship is an important component of a quilt's value. The piecing and appliqué should be taken into account. Do seams meet? Do corners end in crisp points when they are supposed to? Is the appliqué gracefully cut and sewn to form smooth, flawless curves? Is the quilting pattern utilitarian or a visually rich and complex design? Are the quilting stitches small and even? The size of the stitches—measured by the number in each inch—indicates the quilter's skill; tinier stitches mean higher skill.

When a quilt is viewed as a fabric painting, the overall visual impression is more important than the quality of the needlework technique, but in the very best quilts, all the elements of composition and craftsmanship are present in a high state of refinement.

Enjoying Quilts

People respond to quilts on multiple levels. For many people, the primary delight is the interplay of color and pattern. For others, the tactile qualities of the fabric and the stitching are foremost. Students of fabric find the particular use of fabric and types of needlework employed as interesting as the compositional elements. And, on some level, almost everyone who appreciates quilts is reacting in part to the historical or social context of the piece and the long-ago world it evokes.

Quilts, no less than other art objects, hold within them an echo of the time when they were created. Recognition of this is one aspect of quilt appreciation. On the other hand, historical context may give way to purely visual and tactile appreciation. A person who hangs an Amish Center Diamond quilt in a corporate boardroom, for instance, usually sees the quilt as a fabric painting, not a representation of the aesthetic of a devout, reclusive, early 20th-century farming community. It is a testament to the quilt maker's artistic sophistication that her creation can hold its own so effectively, even when so far removed from the context in which it was made.

The test of time is perhaps the truest test of whether or not something is art. Has the piece itself endured and does it compel the viewer to spend time experiencing it and trying to understand it? There is little question that quilts are equal to this challenge. They evoke a complex range of responses in nearly all those who come in contact with them. They offer both comfort and beauty. Whether seen as fabric paintings or as bedcovers, there is room for each viewer to apply his or her own criteria for success. Some value elegant needlework. Others find the most interest and importance in the overall strength of the design. The examples discussed in this book were made over the last 200 years. They are at least as highly valued now as when they were created. What further trial need there be? They have stood the test of time—and triumphed.

A Gallery of Quilts

In the pages that immediately follow, you will find a small gallery of exceptional quilts that trace approximately 100 years of quilt making. These quilts exemplify the finest in artistry, originality, detail, and collectibility. They were labors of love, and they endure as pieces of history.

▲ *Star of Bethlehem quilt,*
origin unknown, c.1840.
The quilt maker chose to
use broderie perse to
embellish this pattern.
100in/2.5m square,
private collection.

▲ *Star of Bethlehem quilt,*
Lancaster County, Penn.,
c.*1860. The star in this*
quilt, made from cotton
crazy patches, is surrounded
by a Bear's Paw pattern.
82in/2.08m square,
author's collection.

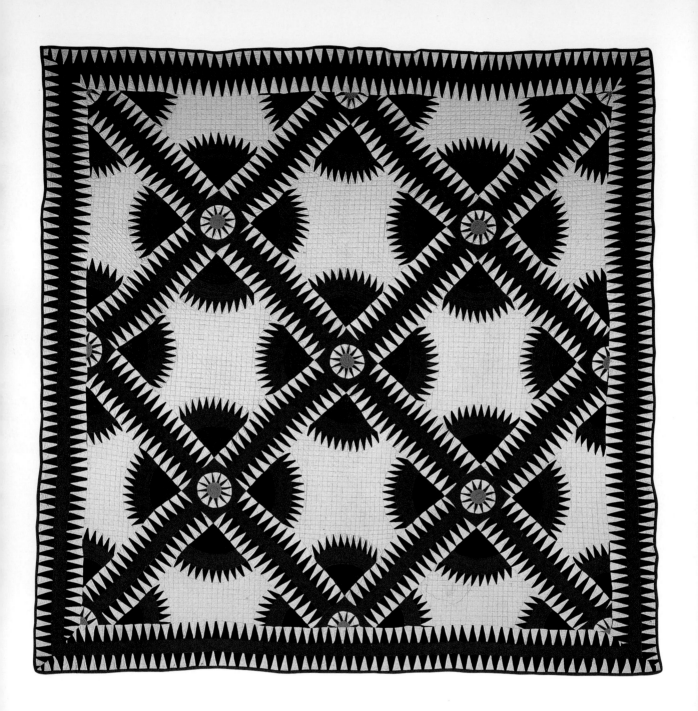

▲ *New York Beauty quilt,*
origin unknown, c.*1870. This*
is a traditional interpretation
of a very bold pattern.
Dimensions unavailable,
private collection.

▲ *Original appliqué quilt,*
Pennsylvania, c.1870. Both
the colors and four-quadrant
format are typical of Eastern
Pennsylvania appliqués of
this period.
86in/2.18m, private
collection.

An American Quilts Primer **31**

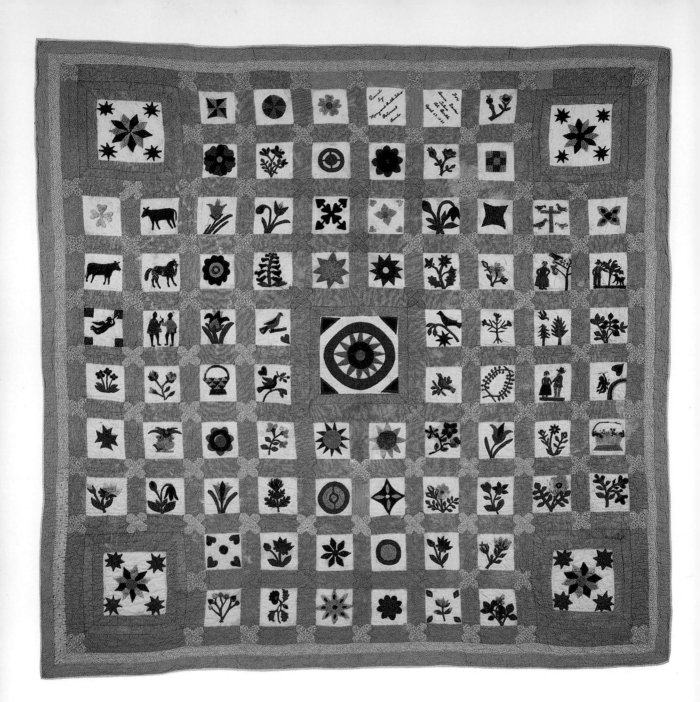

▲ *Mother-daughter Album
quilt, origin unknown,
c.1855–1900. Embroidered on
this quilt is "Pieced by Mary
and Ruth Titus, Paternal
Aunts for Annie Davis Titus
at Birth April 24, 1855."
The top was assembled in the
mid-19th century but quilted
nearly 50 years later.
72in/1.82m, author's
collection.*

▲ *Competitive quilt,*
Lancaster County, Penn.,
c.*1901. One kind of quilt*
contest set quilt makers to
the task of using as many
pieces as possible, a likely
category for this example.
70 x 72in/1.77 x 1.82m,
author's collection.

An American Quilts Primer **33**

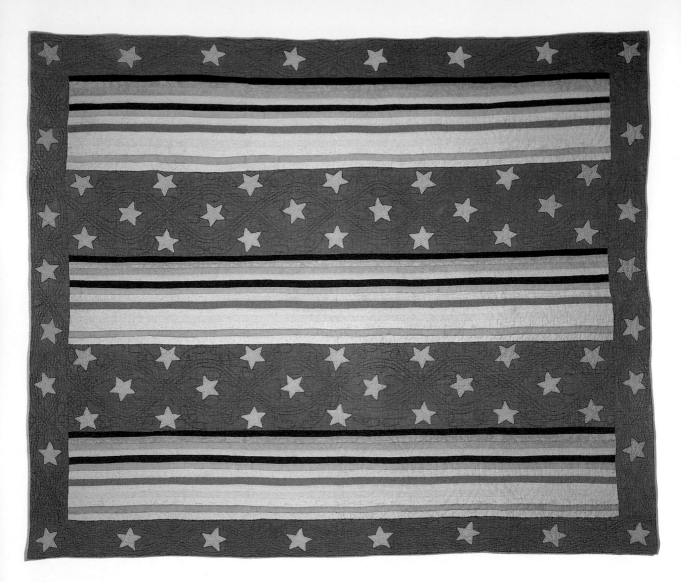

▲ *Patriotic quilt,*
Pennsylvania, c.*1880. This*
quilt could be interpreted as
either an unusual version of
patriotic stars and stripes or
a rainbow against a light
starry sky.
68 x 80in/1.72 x 2.03m,
collection of Michele Fox.

▲ *Patriotic Embroidered*
quilt, Pennsylvania, c.1910s.
The name of each state is
accompanied by an image
of the state's bird, flower, or
symbol. This was probably
created during World War I.
84 x 86in/2.13 x 2.18m,
private collection.

▲ *Birds in Trees quilt,*
origin unknown, c.*1910.*
This whimsical rendition of
the pattern includes details of
a nest with eggs in each tree.
76in/1.93m square, private
collection.

▶ *Pictorial Kit quilt, origin*
unknown, c.*1934. This quilt*
tells the story of "How the
Elephant Got His Trunk,"
from Rudyard Kipling's Just
So Stories. *The pattern and*
all necessary materials were
sold in 1934 for $5. 66 x
80in/1.68 x 2.03m, private
collection.

American Quilt Types

Pieced Center Medallions

Center Medallion quilts consist of a main panel surrounded by a series of borders. The center may be pieced, appliquéd, or made from a single block of printed fabric. Pieced versions, made mostly between 1820 and 1840, incorporate numerous small pieces recycled from clothing, curtains, or bed hangings.

The borders radiate in concentric bands—each successively wider—from the edge of the central panel to the quilt binding. (The top edge that would be covered by the pillows may be either narrower or wider.) The borders, of solid or printed fabrics, pieced or unpieced, provide a frame for the medallion and extend the quilt's size. Some examples alternates pieced and unpieced borders and created other patterns in pieced borders. These patterns were later recast as blocks to form a quilt's entire design.

The makers of Pieced Center Medallion quilts concentrated their efforts on the piecing and overall design. The large number of disparate fabrics made it especially challenging to balance colors. With so much patterning and without a solid white or neutral background, ornamental quilting would have been marginally visible. Many of these quilts are tightly quilted, but typically in simple patterns such as parallel diagonal lines or diamonds.

The use of recycled fabrics accounts for the scarcity of Pieced Center Medallion quilts in mint condition. By the time the fabrics made it into a quilt, many had already withstood 20 or more years of use with varying degrees of resiliency. The quilts themselves were functional pieces subject to further wear—some early examples have survived nearly 200 years. Despite their fragility and the frequent evidence of the ravages of age and use, Pieced Center Medallion quilts are a treasure-trove of early fabrics and are eagerly sought by textile historians and collectors.

John Hewson Panel Quilt, Virginia, c.1790

The plain blue blocks in the outermost pieced border are placed consistently, with matching red fabric on top and bottom.

The printed floral outer borders repeat the theme in the center and unify the design.

The panel is especially well complemented by the deep indigo triangle border.

The color combination is very rich and well balanced, although much of the quilt was likely made from scraps.

Size: 74 x 86in/
1.88 x 2.18m
Value: $20,000+

Stipple Quilt, Maryland, c.1820

The wide variety of fabrics make this quilt of particular interest to collectors. The latest materials date to the 1820s, the earliest from the turn of the 18th century.

Note the irregularity of the piecing in the upper left corner of the blue zigzag border.

The quilting is executed in a technique known as stipple quilting. Patterns of straight lines are used in all but the center panel and the outermost pieced border, where floral forms are used.

The unpieced borders are of fabrics that were made for this purpose or cut down from wider pieces of material.

Size: 78 x 94in/
1.88m x 2.39m
Value: $4,000–$6,000

▶ *This cotton quilt backed with linen is very fine, with beautiful fabrics and excellent quilting. It falls into a lower-value category than the one opposite only because that one includes a center panel made by John Hewson.*

◀ *In this cotton and linen quilt, the center panel was not appliquéd. It was printed by John Hewson specifically to serve as a center medallion. Panels of his work are extraordinarily scarce. This, more than anything, makes this example an important piece.*

Revolutionary Print Maker

John Hewson began his print works in England. In the mid- and late 18th century, England feared losing its textile manufacturing business to its colonies in the New World. To maintain the colonists as customers and forestall their becoming competitors, British law forbade exportation of tools, machinery, and plans for machinery that would make textile production possible.

In 1773, with the assistance of Benjamin Franklin, Hewson and his family moved to Pennsylvania. The following year, he opened a bleaching and printing business in Philadelphia. Hewson was blessed not only with extraordinary talent but also with a prodigious memory. He established his American factory from plans he had memorized in England. The British denounced him as a traitor. Undaunted, Hewson became an American patriot, fighting on the side of his new country in the Revolutionary War.

Hewson's printed fabrics were considered equal to, if not better than, the finest European versions. Among his prints were panels—usually depicting elongated, flower-filled urns surrounded by birds and butterflies—designed as the centers for quilts. He retired in 1810, but his print work was carried on by his son until 1825. Hewson's work is considered unparalleled in the history of printed fabric in this country.

Appliqué Center Medallions

Appliqué Center Medallion quilts are the product of creative resourcefulness. Although considered high-style quilts, their format was developed with cost in mind. Typically, these quilts feature broderie perse chintz appliqué on a white ground. White, unprinted cotton cost less than printed or dyed material. It also formed the perfect setting for the rich colors, images, and patterns of the printed chintz.

Traditionally, chintz is printed with deep-toned, multicolor, large-scale designs of flowers, birds, and blossoming branches. To best use the expensive fabric, quilt makers used an appliqué technique called "Persian embroidery." The quilter cut desired images from the printed fabric and sewed them to the ground fabric. Most often, the appliqués used the images exactly as printed on the fabric. Somtimes, however, quilters combined parts of flowers and leaves and overlapped them to create new forms such as swags or wreaths. Broderie perse appliqué encouraged the creation of innovative, sometimes fanciful, designs that are not possible with pieced work or other styles of appliqué.

Most Center Medallion quilts, whether appliqué or pieced *(see page 40)*, were made between 1820 and 1840. By about 1850, they were supplanted by repeat-block patterns. Most also seem to have originated in urban areas, especially in Philadelphia and Charleston, and were kept as best quilts for special occasions, not used as everyday bedcovers. Generally, a basket of flowers or a floral bouquet served as the central motif, although some excellent examples feature eagles. The floral imagery clearly came from Indian palampores *(see page 99)*.

Quilt makers often attached the appliqué using fine embroidery, did their quilting well, and, in the finest examples, included trapunto *(see page 145)*. These quilts are almost always large. It is not uncommon to find examples that measure 110in/2.8m square.

Quilt collectors who are especially interested in early fabric and quilting prize these quilts. The quilts' practicality is limited in that they are usually too large to hang on walls and too delicate to use as everyday bedcovers. Their beauty, however, and what they reveal about early 19th-century fabrics are unlimited.

Broderie Perse Quilt, Georgia, c. 1825

The colors of the chintz in this quilt are particularly soft and lovely.

Only one fabric is used throughout the body of this quilt; the border is a second fabric. Usually, there are more.

The quilting augments the graceful floral motifs of the chintz appliqué.

Quilted continuous vines surround the two central wreaths.

Size: 96in/2.45m square
Value: $4,000–$6,000

Eagle Medallion Quilt, Frederick, Maryland, *c.*1840

The sunflower adds a lighthearted element to an otherwise formal quilt.

The eagle, star, and green vines with leaves are all done in reverse appliqué—a technique that requires even greater skill than laid work.

Eagles were a popular motif in all types of decorative arts in the Federal period. They were among the earliest freehand appliqué patterns.

The quilting stitches are tiny—18 to the inch (46 per cm).

Size: 96 x 102in/
2.45 x 2.60m
Value: $50,000+

◀ *The overall pattern of this cotton quilt lacks the vibrancy of many examples. The design appears sparse, particularly when compared with the example above.*

▶ *This is the only Crib quilt made by Mrs. Garnhart to have surfaced. The broderie perse central basket is very similar to the baskets on the outer border of the full-size quilt.*

▲ *Anna Catherine Hummel Markey Garnhart was an extraordinary quilt maker who is known to have made at least one quilt for each of her grandchildren. Twelve of her quilts have been located, and several are now in museums. This cotton quilt was as well designed as it was crafted. It is full and well balanced; both the colors and the overall design contribute to the richness of the pattern.*

Whitework Quilts

Whitework quilts are among those that best allowed quilters to show off their needlework. Both the fronts and the backs of these quilts are totally white. The appeal relies on the quality of stitching, the complexity of pattern, and theme's beauty.

Whitework quilts were most popular from 1790 to 1830, although examples from as late as the Civil War era can be found. Typically, the quilts are all cotton. Linen was used in some of the earliest examples, especially for the backing. Their popularity coincided with the interest in Neoclassical themes inspired by the excavation of ancient Roman ruins in the 18th century. American artists and artisans embraced the ideals of purity and simplicity seen in the unearthed architecture and instilled it in their fine and decorative arts and in clothing and furnishings.

In their period, Whitework quilts were called Marseilles work (known today as "stuffed work quilting" or trapunto), a reference to the elaborate, three-dimensional quilting crafted in Provence and then exported through the French port of Marseilles. In stuffed work, the quilter creates high relief by separating threads on the woven back and pushing batting through the tiny opening with a needle. Low relief, used for lines and vines, is made by a technique known as cording, in which yarn is threaded between two closely parallel lines of stitching.

Whitework quilts often employed a central medallion format, with a basket or urn of flowers or an eagle as the motif. Pineapples, the symbol of hospitality, frequently appeared, as did floral wreaths, feathered vines, and grape clusters. Hearts or double sets of initials generally indicate a bridal quilt.

Fine Whitework quilts were considered one of the ultimate expressions of sophisticated and refined taste. In 18th- and 19th-century estate inventories, Whitework quilts were esteemed above all others, although today they tend to be undervalued.

Trapunto Whitework Quilt, origin unknown, c.1825

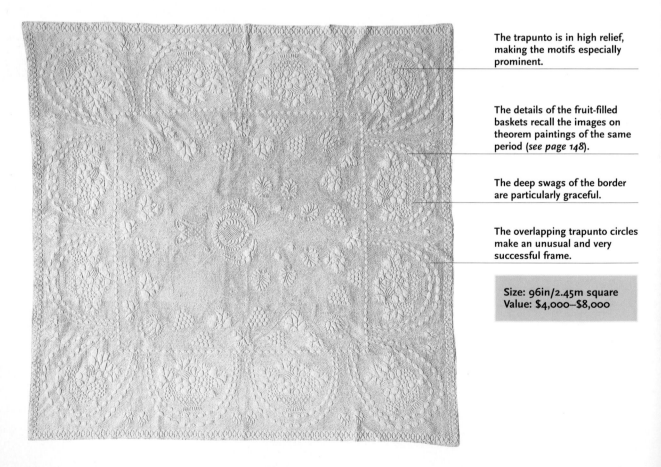

The trapunto is in high relief, making the motifs especially prominent.

The details of the fruit-filled baskets recall the images on theorem paintings of the same period (*see page 148*).

The deep swags of the border are particularly graceful.

The overlapping trapunto circles make an unusual and very successful frame.

Size: 96in/2.45m square
Value: $4,000–$8,000

"Russellville Fair" Quilt, Kentucky, *c.*1856

The images of horses, buildings, barnyard animals, cattle, and human figures are extraordinarily rare in Whitework. The carriages are probably unique.

The central circle shows a judges' tent with several men in full dress.

Circling the tent are saddle and pack horses with grooms and riders, horses pulling carriages, cattle, sheep, and chickens.

More figures of buildings, men, and animals, along with exotic trees, make up the next outermost area.

All is framed by a board fence with two gates.

The overall dimensions of the quilt are increased by the surrounding 4in/10cm fringe.

Size: 86 x 89in/
2.18 x 2.26m
Value: Incalculable

▶ *This cotton quilt is inscribed in quilting that reads: "1856 A REPRE-SENTATION OF THE FAIR GROUND NEAR RUSSELVILLE KENTUCKY." Made by Virginia Mason Ivey in Logan County, Kentucky, it has been in the Smithsonian Institution for the last 50 years, an icon of Americana, and the only known example of a Whitework Pictorial quilt.*

◀ *This cotton quilt's only shortcoming is its weak central motif, which appears too small for the center panel and out of proportion with the border swags. The needlework is very fine, but the design lacks a central important element.*

Whitework or Marseilles?

Be careful not to confuse Whitework quilts with Marseilles spreads. In the late 18th and early 19th centuries, fine, hand-quilted Whitework and commercial versions made on a Jacquard loom were both known as Marseilles work.

Today, the term "Marseilles spread" usually refers to the loomed version. These can also be quite elaborate and often feature a center-medallion format that recalls Whitework. Close examination,

though, reveals that they are not hand-quilted. One telltale sign can usually be found on the edges. The selvedges, in particular, reveal that the finishing was done by loom. Machine-made Marseilles spreads make wonderful bedcovers, but they do not have nearly the value of handiwork.

It took a woman considerable time to complete a fine Whitework piece—a painstaking technique often practiced by candlelight—along with much skill, patience, and perseverance.

Wholecloth Quilts

Wholecloth quilts enjoyed a long period of popularity from the last quarter of the 18th century through the first half of the 19th century. Despite the name, they were rarely made from a single piece of cloth, but rather assembled by seaming together several widths of fabric. When made with glazed chintz or other printed cotton or linen, the ornamental aspect of the quilt was provided by the printed design of the fabric. Quilts of silk or wool were of a solid color, embellished by the patterns of the quilting.

As a rule, it was necessary to purchase material expressly for a Wholecloth quilt in order to secure large enough pieces, a significant expense at the time. Until about 1825, fabric was imported from Europe, some with prints made specifically for the U.S. market, featuring American heroes and battles. In addition, popular pillar prints showed variations of Greek columns with lush flowers and foliage, sometimes including birds.

Wool quilts, too, were made of imported fabric, for American wool was considered too coarse. Expensive to make, Wholecloth quilts were bedcovers for the wealthy. While most quilters used newly purchased fabric, some refashioned bed curtains or used the elaborately quilted petticoats of silk or wool fashionable at the time.

The quilting patterns usually focused on a central motif such as an urn or a basket of flowers, consistent with the patterns used in appliqué in the same era. Around the central motif were elaborate feathers and scrolls. For wool Wholecloth quilts, the most popular color was deep indigo. Shades of green and brown were also used, but the most surprising color was hot pink in a shade so vivid that it is hard to imagine it was available two centuries ago.

Collectors are more likely to find Wholecloth quilts in New England, where many were made, than in other regions. Due to their scarcity, an example in good condition usually brings several thousand dollars.

Silk Wholecloth Quilt, origin and date unknown

The silk, which usually becomes very brittle, has held up well in this quilt: it has remained supple.

The fine quilting is in a center-medallion format typical of solid-color Wholecloth quilts of this period.

There is slight discoloration along a fold line. While minimal, it would be difficult to remove and thus detracts from the quilt's value.

Size: 80 x 88in/
2.03 x 2.24m
Value: $1,200–$2,000

Wholecloth Quilt, New England, *c.*1830

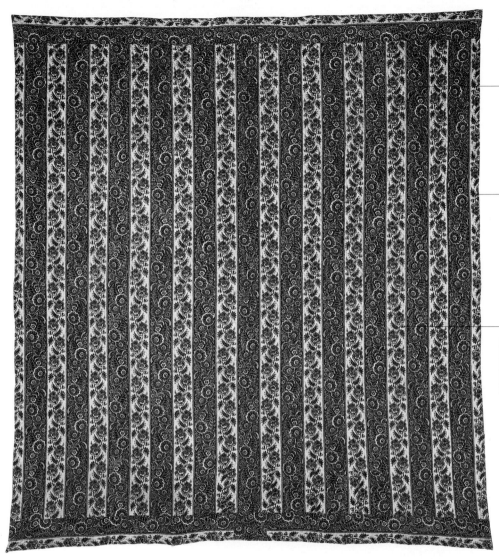

The most unusual feature of this quilt is the use of a printed fabric that appears to have been pieced in strips. Despite this visual effect, it is actually a Wholecloth quilt.

The print and placement of the fabric allow for the appearance of a border at each side with the use of only a single print.

The blue leaves against the lighter part of the fabric add graceful curves to what would otherwise have been a starkly vertical pattern.

Size: 84 x 96in/
2.13 x 2.44m
Value: $2,000–$3,000

▲ *Several pieces of the same cotton fabric were seamed together to produce this Wholecloth quilt.*

◀ *Placement of the seams on this quilt indicates that the fabric had likely seen earlier use as a petticoat before being restyled as a bedcover.*

Four-Poster Quilts

Not all quilts are rectangular or square; some were made in what is now known as the T-shape. This style of bedcover, produced primarily in New England during the first half of the 19th century, came into being because of the popularity of four-poster beds. The sides and foot-end of the quilt were fashioned, essentially, as flaps that fell neatly between the foot posts of the bed.

Collectors who display quilts as wall hangings are reluctant to purchase these, believing that the odd shape is ungainly when viewed on a wall. As bed coverings, however, they continue to be practical and lovely, particularly when used on the type of bed for which they were originally intended. Because of their limited market, they can often be purchased for less than a comparable quilt of standard shape.

Competitive Quilts

Quilt patterns were not published until the mid- to late 19th century. Before that time, state and agricultural fairs were the primary vehicles through which women learned about new patterns and techniques and gained exposure to the work of others. State fairs, which might draw tens of thousands of visitors, often sponsored exhibitions and contests that highlighted needlework and domestic arts. Groups other than agricultural societies also held contests, although records are disappointingly vague when it comes to describing the quilts entered in these competitions. In one popular contest that many fairs promoted, however, entrants vied to make a quilt composed of the most pieces. Certainly not all highly pieced quilts were entered in actual contests, but it seems a reasonable guess that most were made in the spirit of competition. The typeof quilt in focus here is the quilt that makers pieced and designed competitively. Fairs offered prizes and premiums for other types, as well, but those descriptions are even more vague.

Contrary to popular lore concerning quilts that were made thriftily from tiny scraps culled from other projects or snipped from well-worn garments, contest quilts developed without regard to economy. They were carefully designed and crafted to resemble complex mosaics made of hundreds—sometimes thousands—of tiny squares, triangles, and hexagons. Several factors support the conclusion that these quilts were not made from recycled fabrics. For one, the quilts survived in excellent condition. Owners apparently did not use them as everyday bedcovers or launder them frequently. Instead, the quilts were carefully preserved and brought out only for special occasions. In addition, the quilt maker had to have a sufficient array of fabrics to complete the complex design typical of a Competitive quilt—more fabric in more carefully matched colors and patterns than could be found in a scrap bag. Finally, the intricate piecing and fine quilting reveal that the makers had the luxury of time to devote to their creations, a situation most commonly available to people of at least modest means.

Hourglass Quilt, New York State, c.1890

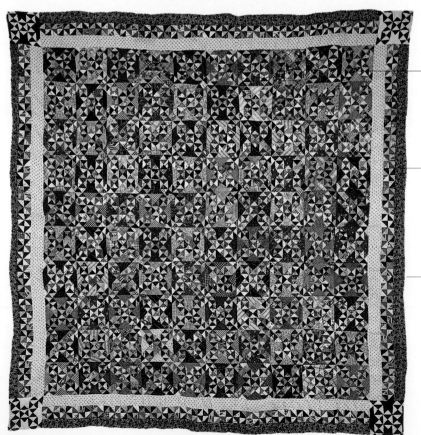

This quilt incorporates several patterns that form an overall crisscross as well as the groupings of triangles within each block

Repeating the hourglasses in the border and the corner blocks adds continuity to this busy pattern.

The design of the pattern is better than its execution. In a quilt with so many pieces, it is extremely difficult to get them all perfectly aligned.

Size: 69 x 72in/
1.75 x 1.83m
Value: $900–$1,400

Pinwheel Quilt, Lancaster County, Pennsylvania, *c.*1880

Every block in this quilt was constructed using the same pattern. However, the quilt maker's choices of fabric colors and prints make the blocks look different from one another.

The zigzag is not commercial rickrack: each section is a fabric strip ⅓ in/1.6cm long and is separately pieced.

The only design variation this quilter made occurs in the center of each block. Most continue the Pinwheel pattern, but a few are single blocks with printed faces *(see detail photo)*.

The quilt maker chose the classic Dutchy color scheme *(see page 155)*. The solid red and yellow used together, as well as the calicoes within each block, are typical Pennsylvania German color choices.

Size: 72in/1.83m square
Value: $10,000+

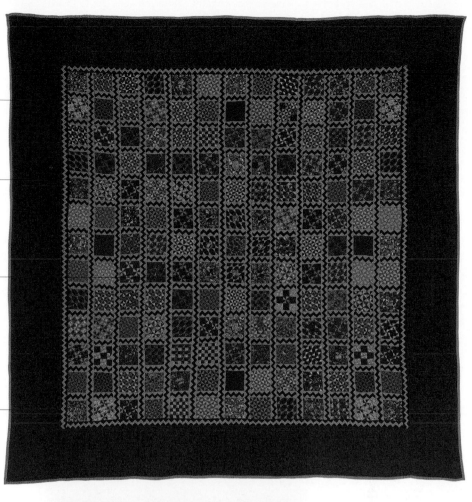

◀ *The edges on this cotton quilt are wiggly, and the corner blocks are uneven in size. Both of these are indications that either the triangles are irregular in size, they were not perfectly sewn together, or both. No documentation exists to verify that this or the example above was actually entered in a contest. Nevertheless, they are the types of quilts women made to show off their piecing and design skills.*

▲ *This quilt is imaginatively and meticulously pieced and designed. It is difficult to imagine piecing a quilt such as this, in which the side of each triangle is only ⅜in/1cm long.*

◀ *Printed fabric with representations of faces substitutes for the triangles in several blocks of the quilt above. This is an extremely unusual variation.*

Friendship Quilts

Friendship quilts are often called Album quilts—and vice versa. In actuality, there is a difference between the two. In a Friendship quilt, the blocks may all be made from the same fabrics or different ones, but the same pattern occurs throughout. In an Album quilt *(see page 52)*, most or all of the blocks use different patterns. (The confusion may be due in part to the fact that many block patterns used in the Friendship quilt, have "Album" in their name—Album, Album Patch, and Album Star, for example.) Because of the repetition of blocks, Friendship quilts generally present less visual drama than Album quilts.

There was no specific pattern or pattern type used for a Friendship quilt. As long as the pattern offered an open center in which a name or verse could be inscribed, the selected pattern could be pieced or appliqué. In parts of Southeastern Pennsylvania and Maryland, appliqué blocks that resemble paper cutouts were popular; they were often rendered in red and white. Other regions favored pieced patterns. The majority of Friendship quilts from the 1840s and 1850s were done in combinations of red and green, a popular palette for all types of quilts at that time. Each

block in the quilt had a signature. When signed in ink, the autograph was written either freehand or using a stencil, with many flourishes. Quilters also might embroider names in cross-stitch or chain stitch. For those unable—or too shy—to create their own verses, magazines offered suggestions with appropriate sentiments.

The fashion for Friendship quilts was at its height in the 1840s and 1850s when the country was in the grip of the idea of Manifest Destiny. Territories were being annexed and the population was on the move. When families left their communities to explore new frontiers, they were often given Friendship quilts to take to their new locations. A social group might also make a Friendship quilt to commemorate a special event, such as a birth or marriage, or, occasionally, as a memorial for someone who had died. (The last would be presented to the family of the deceased.)

The value of Friendship quilts varies greatly, depending upon pattern, complexity, fabrics, and detail of inscriptions. A quilt that gives enough information to trace the specific individuals mentioned is very desirable.

Friendship Chain Quilt, origin unknown, c.1850s–1920s

This pattern, known variously as Friendship Chain, Album Patch, and Chimney Sweep, is popular for use in Friendship quilts.

This quilt's merit is historical rather than aesthetic. All the blocks are inscribed, mostly with verses.

The open center is an ideal ground for signatures and messages.

The pieced pattern and quilting are fairly basic. The donors evidently placed more emphasis on their written sentiments than on their sewing skills.

Size: 94 x 98in/ 2.39 x 2.44m
Value $600–$1,000

Friendship Quilt, Pennsylvania, *c.*1846

This is an unusual pattern, particularly for a Friendship quilt. It resembles a pattern called Bachelor's Puzzle, so perhaps it was made for a marriage.

There is a wonderful variety of red fabrics; nearly every red piece is a unique hue.

The large number of pieces in each block and their graduated sizes make this a more complex pattern than is usually seen in Friendship quilts.

The border—in a different but related pattern to the interior—adds to the complexity of this quilt.

Size: 73 x 84in/
1.85 x 2.13m
Value: $2,500–$3,500

▶ *This cotton quilt has a signature in every block and the date 1846 in one. It is signed "Pennsylvania." The lack of inscriptions leaves us mystified as to its purpose. But the pattern is unusual and finely made, the choice of fabrics adds interest, and it is well designed and in unused condition—all adding to its desirability.*

◀ *This cotton quilt was begun in the 1850s and completed in the 1920s, as indicated by the inscriptions. The quilt is also inscribed with the names of towns in Massachusetts, New Hampshire, and Wisconsin. We know the quilt was made as a departure gift, and the woman for whom it was made was born in New England. Further details are vague.*

Inscriptions from a Farewell Quilt

Oh be thou blest with all that Heaven can send
Long health long youth long pleasures and a friend
Northfield Mass 1850 —Mrs. Joseph P Lee

While sojourning in a land far from your native home, may this simple token remind you of the love of a sister who will ever think of you.
Northfield, Ms. Aug. 19th 1850 —Charlotte H Spyman

May our friendship ever be
Lasting as the Cedar tree
Greenfield, Mass. —Joanna Hinsman

Album Quilts

Album quilts were created as remembrances. One was often made for a community member who was moving away, or to celebrate an important life event, such as marriage. In all cases, Album quilts were intended to maintain a person's connection with his or her community, and they appeared in both rural and urban areas throughout the country. The earliest originated in Maryland and Pennsylvania, but their popularity spread north through New York and New England, west to Ohio and Indiana, and as far south as North Carolina.

Most Album quilt blocks were appliquéd rather than pieced. While quilters predominantly used red and green, some early examples appear in chintz. Typically, one person either made or oversaw production of all the blocks in an effort in ensure uniformity of size. They sometimes made the central, or dedication, block significantly larger than the other blocks, a carryover of the center-medallion format. A competitive aspect may have crept into the creation of Album quilts that did not exist in Friendship quilts, in which each block was the same.

Album quilts frequently included signatures and verses, but other elements may be "read," as well. Appliqué or quilted hearts indicated that the quilt was made for a bride. Wreaths often symbolized an honor of some sort. Flowers had specific meanings—for example, red roses for romantic love, violets for modesty, and white lilies for purity. Compotes of fruit indicated plenty, and doves represented matrimonial happiness. The symbols of fraternal orders sometimes appeared on Album quilts. These symbols may offer clues as to the purpose or person for whom the quilt was made. Often, they raise questions, which is part of the fascination with this quilt form.

The fashion for Album quilts extended from 1840 through the 1870s, when they began to evolve into Crazy quilts. Prices for Album quilts vary significantly, but no others approach the value of those made in Baltimore.

Southern Album Quilt, Georgia, c.1870

These border colors are especially rich when used together and provide a very effective frame for the quilt.

The quilting, a utilitarian crosshatch, does not add decorative richness, thus diminishing the quilt's value.

This example lacks the technical fineness and distinctive detail that add value to such Album quilts as the example opposite.

The blocks include an interesting assortment of traditional and original patterns.

Size: 86 x 90in/
2.18 x 2.29m
Value: $2,000–$3,000

Album Quilt by Ruth Penn, Maryland, *c.*1850

The swag border is a wonderful continuation of the curved lines and forms used throughout the quilt.

The quilting continues the botanical theme of the appliqué.

Using four urns for the center blocks adds unity to the overall composition.

The signatures on this quilt (not visible here), especially the explicit detailed provenance, add to its desirability.

Size: 80 x 100in/
2.03 x 2.54m
Value: $8,000–$18,000

◀ *The teal and chestnut borders seen here are unusual for an Album quilt. This color scheme is more prevalent in Southern quilts than in those made elsewhere, but few documented examples of Southern Albums exist. This quilt's rarity compensates for the somewhat pedestrian execution of the style.*

▶ *The use of related but different urns and flowers for each of the center blocks adds to this quilt's visual interest.*

▲ *Ruth Penn made this quilt for her son Robert on the occasion of his marriage. The craftsmanship here is especially fine. In addition to the appliqué, Penn provided detail through the use of embroidery and reverse appliqué. Ruching, a strip of pleated fabric or trim such as lace, is used to make one of the yellow and red flowers three-dimensional. (This technique is rarely seen outside of Baltimore Album quilts.)*

Baltimore Album Quilts

Baltimore Album quilts are considered the epitome of design and technique. As with Album quilts *(see pages 52–53)*, they were usually made as keepsake gifts. But the term "Baltimore Album" refers to a specific type of quilt, made primarily of appliqué blocks, that flourished in Baltimore for a mere 6 years (1846–52). A true Baltimore Album meets two criteria: if its provenance is known (it can be documented that it was made in Baltimore during this period); and/or if it contains the distinctive blocks of one of the three professional quilt makers responsible for the most elaborate blocks. Three hundred Baltimore Album quilts have been documented.

The only maker known by name is Mary Simon, a German who arrived in Baltimore in 1844; the others are recognized only by their unique styles of blocks. Mrs. Simon's work is characterized by layered appliqué. Hers appears to be the only work that includes white roses, blue triple bowknots, and elaborate baskets. She also created remarkably detailed human figures in full clothing.

Baltimore Album quilts may contain a combination of professionally made and homemade blocks, many of which bear signatures. Recent research indicates that a name generally refers to a person who purchased a particular block. Blocks could be purchased with the appliqué motifs either completed or basted in position and ready to be finished by the quilt's presenters. The motifs were most often floral, but they also included images of people, birds, or animals; Bibles or cornucopias; or sailing ships or landmark buildings. Fine details, such as thorns on roses, were embroidered. The appliqué was simple, layered, or stuffed, according to the maker's skill and artistic preference.

Because cotton production was Baltimore's largest industry at the time, makers chose from a much broader range of fabrics than found elsewhere, including unusual rainbow fabrics, especially in shades of blue, and chintz. Baltimore Album quilts have sold for upwards of $200,000, which makes the distinction between a verified Baltimore Album and a generic example especially important.

Commemorative Baltimore Quilt, *c.*1850

In addition to the flat appliqué, there is stuffed appliqué, reverse appliqué, and embroidery. Additional detail is drawn with ink.

Unusual fabrics were carefully cut and sewn to provide realistic detail, such as the steps of the buildings, leaves, and fruit.

This quilt is in unwashed condition, and the colors are unusually vibrant.

Several blocks have images that refer to then-current events. The log cabin and cider barrel were popular motifs left over from the 1840 and 1844 presidential campaigns by the Whig Party.

The use of red lozenge shapes in the border, rather than a traditional sawtooth, effectively carries through the curved forms used throughout the body of the quilt.

The railroad car commemorates the new, fast steam engines that had their inaugural runs from Baltimore in 1837.

Size: 106 x 107 in/
2.70 x 2.72m
Value: $150,000+

Baltimore Monument Quilt, c.1845

These patterns are graceful and well rendered, but lack the extraordinarily elaborate, layered appliqué that catapults a Baltimore Album quilt's value.

The nine central blocks create a subpattern that is very well balanced.

The center block's architectural details were skillfully created with printed fabric, probably by professional quilters.

This central block is a different rendition of the monument in the top left block of the quilt on the facing page.

Size: 77in/
1.96m square
Value: $15,000–$25,000

▶ *This cotton quilt, signed and dated "M.R. Horn 1893," descended in the family of T. Rowe Price in Baltimore. The style of the fabrics, however, indicates that the quilt was made 50 years earlier, then presented as a gift a second time in 1893.*
The Battle Monument depicted in the central block honors 39 Baltimore citizens who died in the War of 1812. With more squares such as this one, the quilt would bring a higher price. Images of buildings, animals, and people make an Album quilt more collectible .

◀ *The richness of this cotton quilt, inscribed "Sarah Poole and Mary J. Poole," is virtually unparalleled. With the exception of three fairly simple red and green renditions, all the blocks include superb detail and were likely designed and executed by professional quilt makers.*

William Rush Dunton

Dr. William Rush Dunton was a psychiatrist in Maryland. Interested in occupational therapy, Dr. Dunton believed that the concentration required to create quilts and the shared activity of making them were beneficial to the mental health of his "nervous ladies." He was so enthusiastic about the benefits and appeal of quilting that he wrote a book, which was published in 1946, called *Old Quilts*.

In his book, Dr. Dunton described many quilts in great detail, particularly Baltimore Album quilts, and speculated about the existence of a professional quilt maker he believed had created the finest examples. The information available to Dr. Dunton led him to conclude that the maker was Mary Evans Ford. Although Dr. Dunton's intentions were good, his conclusions misled researchers for many years.

Recent research indicates that the designer of many of the finest Baltimore Album blocks was Mary Simon. Given the number of examples located that use her blocks, however, it seems impossible that Mrs. Simon—a young mother during the period when the blocks were created—actually completed each quilt personally. The time required to produce such volume precludes it. Instead, researchers believe she designed the blocks as a kind of part-time job and sold them in basted or sewn form.

Sampler Quilts

Like Album quilts, Sampler quilts were made with a different pattern in each block. The two types of quilts are similar in appearance, but they differ in terms of the quilt makers' intent. Some served the same teaching purpose as needlework samplers, but others were made much later in life, closer in spirit to Friendship or Album quilts (see pages 50 and 52). Sometimes a quilt maker created a commemoration in quilted form, saving a block from each quilt she had made in the past, or using the practice blocks from quilts she intended to make. In addition to creating a sampler of quilt patterns, some makers displayed different quilting styles in each block.

The patterns in a Sampler quilt tend to be pieced, rather than appliqué, although this is by no means a hard rule. In a true Sampler each block presents a different pattern, and in some cases, a different size as well. Sampler quilts may or may not have sashing that separates the blocks. It is not uncommon to find a Sampler quilt in which each block directly abuts the next. While Album quilts frequently have one or more dates, Samplers generally have none. Album quilts are also more likely to show occasional repeated blocks.

Collectors seek Sampler quilts for their visual interest as well as their rarity. Fewer Sampler quilts than Albums were made, although it is sometimes a subjective call as to which is which. Since Sampler quilts often served as learning tools, a young quilter had the opportunity to try many patterns, and the variety and juxtaposition of patterns in the finished quilt could be quite engaging. There is also the charm, similar to that of Doll quilts (see page 74), of seeing the earnest first efforts of a budding craftswoman. Some collectors dislike the haphazard effect created when the blocks are dissimilar sizes, but that, again, is a matter of taste. Prices for Sampler quilts are influenced by factors such as the number of blocks, fineness of patterns, arrangement of blocks, and choices of fabric.

Salinda Rupp Quilt, Lancaster County, Pennsylvania, c.1870

The printed red blocks placed between the pieced squares add regularity to what might otherwise appear as a disjointed pattern.

The quilt is made with fabrics typically used in Eastern Pennsylvania in the last quarter of the 19th century. These combinations of patterned fabric and color are not seen anywhere else.

Many of the patterns are quite unusual, and in some cases, multipatterned.

Each block is uniform in size and extremely well pieced.

The diminutive scale of many of the patterns is exceptional.

The zigzag border makes a wonderful enclosure.

Size: 88in/2.24m square
Value: $20,000+

Eccentric Sampler Quilt, Evansville, Indiana, c.1930s

Many of the patterns are traditional, but several are well out of the ordinary.

Typical of many Sampler quilts, the blocks are of varying sizes.

The quilt maker has carried pieces of the same fabrics throughout the quilt, creating some cohesiveness within an otherwise random design.

The maker was very resourceful in using small patterns to fill in the uneven spaces.

This quilt is not finely crafted, which diminishes its value, but it has a buoyancy that is appealing.

Size: 70 x 88in/
1.78 x 2.24m
Value: $700–$1,000

▶ The disparate sizes of the blocks suggest that this cotton quilt was made either from saved blocks or practice blocks. On the other hand, the same fabrics are used throughout, all consistent with the 1930s. This would point to their having been made over a relatively short period, perhaps for this quilt.

◀ This quilt falls at the opposite end of the Sampler spectrum from the quilt above. Undoubtedly, the blocks were created specifically for this quilt. In some, the maker used an additional pattern within the overall block, leading to some very creative combinations. It is stenciled with the name of the maker, Salinda Rupp.

Mother-Daughter Quilts

The term "mother-daughter quilt" does not refer to family ties. It relates purely to the discrepancy in age seen between some quilt tops and their backings. It is not uncommon to find that a quilt top was appliquéd or pieced in one generation and the quilting finished in another. Such quilts are generally less desirable to collectors than one from a single era.

In instances in which the more recent fabrics and quilting are compatible with the older part, the quilt's other features—its workmanship and artistic elements—may ameliorate or overcome the inconsistency. Quilts that have been completed with glaringly out-of-period materials—a 19th-century top, for instance, with synthetic batting—are of little interest to the collector.

As in all decisions about which quilts to collect, a great deal of subjectivity comes into play. What one purchaser may find acceptable, another may not. Find out whether the quilt was assembled at one time. If not, the price should reflect the disparity.

Strip Quilts

The term "Strip quilt" does not refer to a specific pattern but rather to the way the pattern pieces are assembled—the set—which strongly influences the overall design. The center-medallion format *(see pages 40–43)* is one example of a set. Beginning in about 1840 and continuing even today, the repeated-block format predominates as a set.

The strip set, with its long, pieced or unpieced rectangular blocks, was as well known as these sets but used less frequently. Even so, throughout the history of American quiltmaking, there have been individuals and communities that used this format quite effectively. The Bars type of Lancaster County Amish quilt *(see page 78)* is a simple form of Strip quilt. Many quilts attributed to African-American quilt makers use this set, a tradition that may derive from the strip-woven cloth made in West Africa *(see page 84)*.

In its most basic form, a Strip quilt consists of parallel bars or bands of fabric arranged vertically, horizontally, or diagonally. The strips span the entire length or width of the quilt. In more complex examples, the strips are pieced with four patches or nine patches and set either square (the edges of the patches are parallel to the edges of the strip) or on point (the patch is rotated 45° so that, for example, a square looks like a diamond). Pieced strips can be separated by unpieced strips or placed directly next to one another. Some pieced strips are established patterns with standardized names. Wild Goose Chase *(see page 104)* is a strip made of triangles; a strip composed of narrow horizontal patches is recognized as Chinese Coins.

Strip quilting offered a frugal quilt maker the opportunity to use quantities of fabric scraps; some made strip backings for their quilts, even when the fronts were unrelated. In general these quilts were utilitarian efforts, and the quilting was sturdy rather than fine. The Lancaster Amish Bars quilts are consistent exceptions to this.

Precedents for the American Strip quilt are found in numerous English quilts known as "strippies." Typically, the English versions are made with solid-color or printed bars and are not pieced. The quilting is often more elaborate than in American examples. A great many Strip quilts were made in Pennsylvania, by the Amish and others.

Herringbone Strip Quilt, Ohio, c.1890

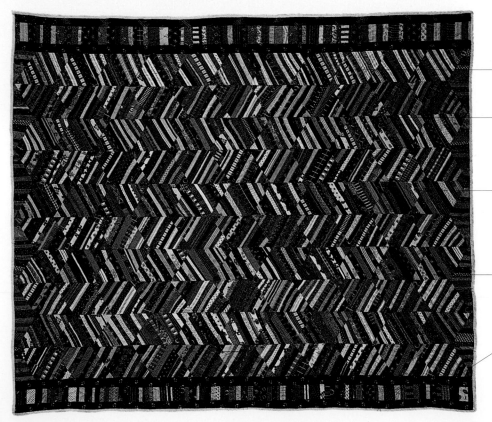

The use of multiple, complex patterns makes for a dazzling whole. When looked at vertically, tumbling blocks appear.

When looked at horizontally, the quilt forms a herringbone pattern.

Each of the strips running from end to end of the quilt is actually made of diamond-shaped blocks that are filled with narrow strips of fabric.

Fabrics are used well to evenly distribute light and dark. The particular placement of light fabrics in contrast to dark adds to the overall sense of movement—an asset.

The Chinese Coins border adds another Strip variation. Unfortunately, the maker didn't feel the need for a frame on all four sides of the quilt.

Size: 70 x 80in/
1.78 x 2.03m
Value: $1,200–$2,400

Hourglass Strip Quilt, New York State, c.1860

The choice of hourglasses, or bow ties, within the dark bars is an unusual variation.

The quilting is better than usual for this type of pattern. The solid-color bars are quilted in a cable pattern, the border in chevrons.

Although a highly subjective call, some collectors would say that the width of the solid-color bars overwhelms the alternate rows.

The hourglasses do not line up.

Size: 60 x 72 in/
1.52 x 1.83m
Value: $800–$1,600

▶ *The piecing in this cotton quilt is a little irregular. While this adds interest and casual charm, it was probably not the maker's intention.*

◀ *This cotton quilt, c.1890, was made in Ohio. This quilt is very well pieced but not finely quilted. In this type of quilt, the quilting tends to be secondary, for it hardly shows between the multiple printed fabrics and pieced patterns.*

Setting a Quilt

The method by which a quilt's subunits are assembled is called the "set" of the quilt. There are four major sets that define quilt designs: medallion, block, all-over pattern, or strip. But within those larger designs, the experienced quilt maker may refer, as well, to the set of the individual blocks.

Generally, blocks are set square, on-point, or diagonal. When the edges of the block are parallel to the edges of the quilt, they are set square, or straight *(see page 74)*. If a block is rotated 45 degrees, so that the square

is a diamond, it is set on-point. On-point settings are sometimes offset to form a zigzag design *(see top of page 73)*. In a diagonal set, the blocks are first sewn together to form a strip, then the strip is sewn into the quilt top at a 45-degree angle to the quilt's edges *(see page 147)*.

The set of the quilt is the first of a quilt maker's many choices. Like other aspects—fabric, color, complexity, stitching—it offers the creator an opportunity to make a piece that, when all the separate choices combine, is individually satisfying.

Victorian Crazy Quilts

The Victorian taste for embellishment reached new heights in these elaborate, highly ornamented, zealously individualistic quilts. Crazy quilts have been called the quintessential pattern of the last quarter of the 19th century, although, strictly speaking, the blocks are not made from a standardized pattern but rather from a harmonious hodgepodge of irregularly shaped patches. The best crazies are made from scraps of silk, satin, and velvet. When set against a dark background such as navy, black, or maroon velvet, the richly colored fabrics glow like stained glass. These elegant fabrics were typical of those used to make dresses for women who were subject to the dictates of Victorian society. Consequently, textile historians assume that these quilts were made in cities where women dressed more formally, rather than in rural areas were clothing was more utilitarian.

The makers of Crazy quilts disdained simple quilting in favor of a lavish array of ornamental stitches and pictorial embroidery. Stitching disguised the seams between the patches; embroidery added richness—and delightful surprises—to the visual feast. The embroidered images might be freehand or from a purchased pattern that could be sewn or transferred to the quilt by ironing. The most popular motifs were flowers, birds, animals, insects, spider webs, and fans. The pictures may also have been painted, rather than sewn, and these could also be freehand or store-bought. Some examples were further adorned with beads and buttons, flat and commemorative ribbons, or glittering metallic threads.

For many years, Victorian Crazy quilts were not greatly sought after by collectors. In the last 5 to 10 years, however, an appreciation of their haphazard aesthetic has been growing. It is difficult to use a Crazy quilt on a bed, however. Many Crazy quilts were made as parlor throws and are too small to serve as bedcovers. In addition, the fabrics, particularly the silk, make them especially fragile. A century-old Crazy could not stand up to the constant handling a bedcover endures, and folding or draping the quilt can also damage the fabrics. A Victorian Crazy quilt in pristine condition is a rare find. To ensure the longevity of one of these little gems, one should have a professional textile restorer make any necessary repairs, then provide it with a good support, and display it on a wall.

Velvet and Satin Crazy Quilt, Pennsylvania, dated 1884

The peacock and the harlequin-garbed child stand out amid the more typical Victorian motifs, such as Japanese fans, strawberries, crescent moons, butterflies, flowers, and birds.

The embroidered dedication to Mama is an endearing grace note.

The border treatment of blocks overlapping the main part of the quilt is unusual. Although its novelty is a plus, its execution is a little clumsy.

Size: 76 x 80in
1.93 x 2.03m
Value: $1,000–$2,000

Velvet, Silk, and Satin Crazy Quilt, New York, dated 1886

Many of the images are three-dimensional, further adding to this quilt's masterpiece status.

The quilt is a veritable menagerie. Some of the animal images—the butterflies, owls, and birds—are typical of Victorian Crazy quilts; but swimming turtles, cows, a camel, and an elephant are far more unusual.

The border of three-dimensional flowers and vines sets off the interior of the quilt.

Two romping cherubs and a gloved hand in high relief holding a scarf add a playful quality to the quilt.

Size: 62 x 72in/
1.56 x 1.83m
Value: $25,000+

◀ *The work on this quilt is all very well done. If the individual pieces were smaller, however, the overall effect would be more graceful.*

▲ *This remarkable quilt was made by Florence Elizabeth Marvin in Brooklyn, New York. If the Victorians believed that more is better, then this must be the best. It is difficult to imagine a Crazy quilt with a greater number of detailed images. No image is repeated.*

◀ *Notice the variety of subjects and the minute attention to detail in the choice of fabrics, stitching, and embroidery. No flourish was left unexecuted.*

Wool Crazy Quilts

Wool Crazy quilts are the countrified versions of Victorian Crazies. They became popular toward the end of the Crazy quilt fad and continued throughout the first quarter of the 20th century. The material in Wool Crazies often came from men's suiting fabrics. The grays, blacks, and navy blues have an understated, companionable elegance, and some Crazies add enlivening splashes of reds and other bright colors. These quilts are embellished with embroidery that follows and emphasizes the seams joining the patches, but in more restrained stitching than in Victorian Crazies. The makers also steered clear of the painted decorations and sewn floral or figural motifs seen on the Victorians.

Wool Crazies can be either quilted or tied. Tied versions had different names in various regions of the country. In most places, people called them comforts, or comforters; Pennsylvanians more often called them haps; Texans referred to them as suggans. When these Crazies are quilted, the work tends to be crude, because the thickness of the fabrics makes fine stitching nearly impossible. More often than not, these quilts do not have border treatments. The pattern goes to the edges of the quilt.

Collectors who prefer dazzling needlework have often overlooked these quilts; but Wool Crazies make up for simple stitching with artistry and design. The placement of shapes and the color combinations in Wool Crazy quilts often create the impression of aerial landscapes. When seeing these Crazies as fabric collages, the quilt enthusiast can appreciate the successful works of design they often are. Wool Crazies are among the most affordable one-of-a-kind quilts available and have considerable appeal to those looking for colorful decoration without huge expense.

Borderless Crazy Quilt, Pennsylvania, c.1900

Had the maker continued the use of red or pink for all the centers, the pattern would have appeared more unified, adding to the quilt's value.

This quilt reveals a nice use of lights and darks.

Even though there is only one type of embroidery stitch used throughout, it provides nice detail and contrast to the large blocks of color.

The quilter used different color threads, but stayed with the herringbone stitch in the same scale throughout. This helps to unify the overall design.

Size: 71in/1.8m square
Value: $400–$700

Star Crazy Quilt, Pennsylvania, *c.*1890

In the corners, matching four-point stars serve to anchor a very busy pattern.

Two small, nine-patch blocks and three blocks with bright red centers evoke the tradition of the Log Cabin pattern. (In Log Cabin, the red center represents the fire on the hearth, *see page 108.*)

The central motif is composed of four blocks, each with a four-point star.

The rays of the central stars form two secondary patterns—a large circle surrounding a star composed of four diamonds.

Size: 82 x 86in/
2.08 x 2.18m
Value: $2,000–$3,000

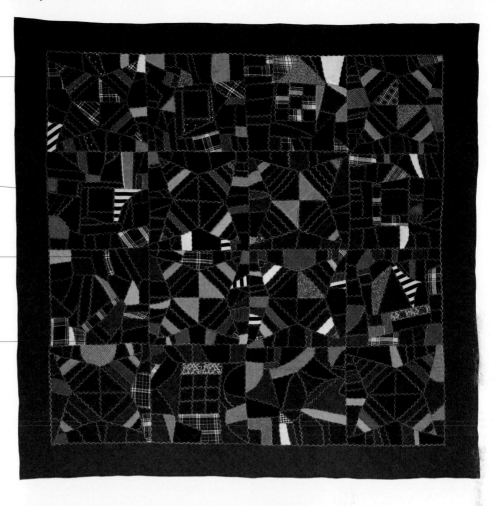

◀ *The large dimensions of the fabric scraps can be a detriment, but in this example the shapes and colors are well placed and lead your eye equally to all parts of the quilt.*

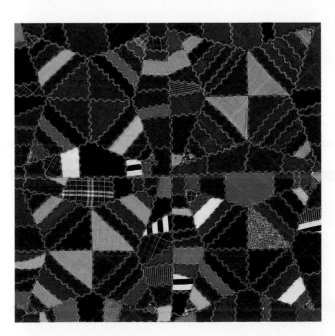

▲ *The construction of this wool Crazy is better than most. It is quilted rather than tied and has a border. It also has the virtue of not being overly bulky.*

◀ *The four central blocks combine to form patterns much like those in a kaleidoscope. There is a four-pointed star in each block, as well as a large elongated four-pointed star in the center, surrounded by a circle.*

Show Quilts

The Centennial Exposition held in Philadelphia in 1876 exposed American visitors to Oriental design for the first time, and they were captivated by what they saw. At the same time, the ideals of the Aesthetic movement—with its emphasis on beautifying the home in order to raise the morality of its inhabitants—began to gain purchase. Virtually every type of household object was decorated in some way in accordance with the belief that more pattern meant more beauty, which meant greater edification. A distinct preference for intricate designs with primary and secondary patterning erupted and swept the nation, affecting quilt styles as much as any other art. Art schools for women arose to teach the range of what was known as "art needlework."

Traditional pieced and appliqué quilts continued to be made in rural areas but became unfashionable in the cities. Sophisticated urban taste disdained calico quilts and prized commercially loomed Marseilles spreads *(see page 45)*. Two forms of elaborately patterned quilts evolved: Victorian Crazy quilts *(see page 60)* and Show quilts. Show quilts share many characteristics with Victorian Crazies, including their popularity span. They were made beginning in the 1870s and were considered passé by the late 1890s. Unlike Crazy quilts, Show quilts came from traditional patterns, but were rendered in silk, satin, fine wool, or velvet, and usually heavily embellished. Block patterns such as Fan, Log Cabin, or Tumbling Blocks enjoyed particular popularity, but any design could be used. Regardless of the specific pattern, the quilts involved complex designs with a lot of movement and layers of patterning. The embroidered images, both purchased and homemade, often included the newly fashionable Oriental motifs. Nineteenth-century Show and Crazy quilts used a great deal of black. This made a dramatic background for the embroidered work.

Many Show quilts are tied, or tufted, rather than quilted. When Show quilts were quilted, the quilters often used thread in a contrasting color that further enriched the surface decoration.

A Show quilt was usually placed on the top of a bed over a Marseilles spread or used as a parlor throw, so these quilts tend to be smaller than bed size. In other words, they were made for show rather than for warmth.

Roman Stripe Show Quilt, origin unknown, *c.*1880s

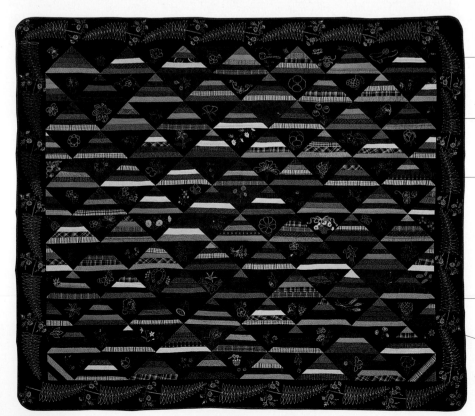

The pattern has tremendous diagonal, as well as vertical and horizontal, movement.

The black triangles forming the lower half of each diamond provide depth against the multicolor strips.

The curved shapes of the embroidered designs are a nice contrast to the straight lines of the pieced patterns.

The embroidered fern border is exceptional. Not only is the theme unusual, but also, the fronds are placed in such a way as to create a graceful, curved frame around the quilt. The contrasting color with which it is sewn makes it more outstanding.

Motifs such as the ear of corn and the shoe add a whimsical note.

70 x 74in/
1.78 x 1.88m
Value: $3,500–$4,500

Fan Show Quilt, origin unknown, *c.*1880

The arrangement of the fans gives this quilt a tremendous amount of movement. Initially, it appears that the fans are swirling every which way around the entire surface. In reality, they alternate very regularly in each block.

The use of white thread makes the quilting very prominent.

The quilting was done by machine. Sewing machines were still a novelty when this quilt was made and many quilt makers were proud to show off that they owned them.

Size: 70in/1.78m square.
Value: $1,500–$2,500

▶ *This wool quilt is well crafted and designed. The sole drawback is that it does not have the elaborate, detailed embroidery that usually characterizes Show quilts. It does, however, have the movement and dramatic design that are typical features of this type of quilt.*

◀ *This wool quilt illustrates all the representative features of a Show quilt: a traditional pattern interpreted in an elegant fabric, a black background to highlight elaborate embroidery, unusual motifs, and strong color and visual movement.*

Development of the Sewing Machine

Sewing machines were developed in the early 19th century. However, it was not until 1846, when Elias Howe thought to move the needle's eye from the blunt end of the needle to the sharp tip, that the sewing machine became a practical tool.

As with many technical innovations, the new machine was at first out of the financial reach of most families. In 1856, however, Howe teamed up with a marketing genius named Isaac Singer, and together they successfully mass-marketed sewing machines. In 1876, their company sold 262,136 machines.

Owning a sewing machine and knowing how to operate it became a status symbol. Although appliqué and quilting continued to be done by hand, it became commonplace for women to piece quilt tops and attach bindings at least partially by machine. When quilting was done on a machine, the quilter often used thread in a contrasting color to make it more visible. It is as challenging to quilt well by machine as by hand. Although today's collector is inclined to discount machine quilting, he or she will best appreciate machine work in the context in which it was done.

Patriotic Quilts

Prior to receiving suffrage in 1920, women expressed their political sentiments and commemorated allegiance to their local and national communities in whatever ways were open to them. Patriotic quilts were one of those ways. Civic-minded quilt makers created the quilts in times either of national threat or celebration. Many were made when the nation was at war, and the quilts' imagery offers a good guide to their dates of origin.

During the War of 1812, many quilts featured eagles similar to the one depicted on the Great Seal of the United States. A remarkable consistency exists among the many 19th-century examples, yet we have no records of eagle patterns having been published. Textile historians assume that a pattern derived from the Great Seal was circulated among groups of women, if not published.

Images of flags and stylized versions of stars and stripes appeared frequently at the time of the Civil War. Even so, the number of stars on a flag does not provide conclusive evidence of when the quilt was made. Women commonly included flag-like symbols, choosing the numbers of stars

to fit their artistic visions, rather than realistically rendering particular flags. Similarly, images of George Washington, especially those on printed fabrics, do not usually date from his lifetime. Most commemorative fabrics showing Washington were made for the 1876 Centennial. The Spanish-American War in 1898 and the two world wars in the 20th century also generated Patriotic quilts.

In the 20th century, political candidates and causes spurred the making of many quilts. Numerous quilts from the 1930s include the initials "NRA," referring to the National Recovery Administration that was established during Franklin Roosevelt's administration (not the National Rifle Association of today). More recently, the Bicentennial Celebration and the Gulf War prompted American expressions of national pride through quilting.

Patriotic quilts cover a vast range in terms of their quality. Regardless, their rarity and individuality make them of interest to collectors. They are hardly ever valued for less than $1,000. More often, they sell for a minimum of several thousands.

Pray for Peace Quilt, origin unknown, c.1940

The stylized flags make wonderful corner blocks.

The maker has repeated the stars, albeit crudely worked, in the quilting. The crude nature of the craftsmanship detracts from the quilt's relative value.

Using red between the arms emboldens the image; the overall color placement adds drama to the Lone Star pattern.

Size: 60in/1.52m square
Value: $2,000–$3,000

Susan B. Anthony Quilt, origin unknown, *c.*1912

Embroidered sayings across the top—"Peace be Thine," "Let Liberty Reign," and "Love Thy Neighbor as Thyself," among others—underscore the patriotic message of the flag.

The quilting, done by both hand and machine, is secondary to the overall design.

The quilt has a crocheted edge that seems to be an attempt at softening the very strong overall pattern. In actuality, it adds little, for the quilt's design success lies in the strong overall image.

Size: 72in/1.83m square
Value: $25,000+

◀ *The workmanship in this cotton quilt lacks the expertise evident in many quilts, but the maker has strongly conveyed her sense of patriotism. The message "Pray for Peace," which related to World War II, adds poignancy to the quilt.*

▲ *This cotton quilt could be classified as a Fundraising example, as well as a Patriotic one, but its significance lies in more than the strong, abstract depiction of the flag. It bears the name of Susan B. Anthony, one of the leaders of the Woman's Suffrage movement. Anthony's name as one of the contributors gives it substantial historical importance and rare value.*

▶ *This is an example of one of the patriotic fabrics made at the time of the Centennial. George Washington on horseback, Liberty bells, and the Declaration of Independence were other popular images.*

Fundraising Quilts

Throughout the history of our country, quilts have been more than mere bedcovers. They have conveyed political messages, celebrated national events, and raised money for worthy causes. Visually and functionally, the first Fundraising quilts were no different from any other quilts; their sole distinction was that they were auctioned or raffled off and the money from the sales donated to a cause. Many times, the buyer gave the quilt back to the charity so it could be resold at another location—thereby preserving the principal, as well as promoting the principles.

Shortly before the Civil War, the fashion changed. For a donation (usually 10 cents), a person could have his or her name, or the name of a business, placed on the quilt. Names were inscribed either in ink or embroidery. The quilt would have been a pieced pattern to which names were added, or the pattern would have been created solely from the placement of the names. When pieced, quilt makers typically used a wheel pattern and wrote the names between the spokes. A larger donation (usually 25 cents) entitled the donor to the most prominent position at the hub of the wheel.

During the Civil War, women of both the Union and the Confederacy sold quilts to raise money for hospital supplies and gunboats, and to support the families of soldiers. In the 1870s, the Women's Christian Temperance Union made quilts to support their effort to persuade men to abstain from alcohol, tobacco, and other intoxicants. They also directed efforts toward reducing the workday to 8 hours, attaining women's suffrage, and establishing equal pay for equal work. Much of their work in the last quarter of the 19th century was subsidized by the quilts they made and sold *(see page 128)*.

Ladies' Aid societies raised money for church and community projects, as well as for disaster relief throughout the world. During World War I, the Red Cross raised money through quilt making. Throughout the 20th century, Mennonite groups held enormous quilt sales, the proceeds of which went to support needy groups around the globe.

Most Fundraising quilts sell for fairly modest amounts; several thousand dollars is the high end of the scale. They are of historical interest, but they are rarely well crafted or artistically complex.

Pieced-Pattern Quilt, Ghent, New York, c.1870

Aside from being a Fundraising quilt, this is a most unusual and interesting pieced pattern.

The names are written in ink. The handwriting is the same within each group of names. Most likely, the person who collected the donations also signed the quilt.

Indigo and white make a very desirable color scheme, regardless of pattern.

Size: 80 x 94in/ 2.03 x 2.39m
Value: $2,000–$3,000

Wheel-Pattern Quilt, Lebanon, Pennsylvania, dated 1933

Names included in the border may be the names of the makers. It would be interesting to know if that is the case here, as the border includes many male names. Perhaps in this quilt, the border was for the major donors.

The wheel pattern, created solely by embroidery, lacks the complexity and interest of a pieced version of the pattern.

This quilt would have more significance, and fetch a higher price, if it provided an indication of the cause for which it was made.

Size: 75 x 88in/
1.90 x 2.24m
Value: $500–$800

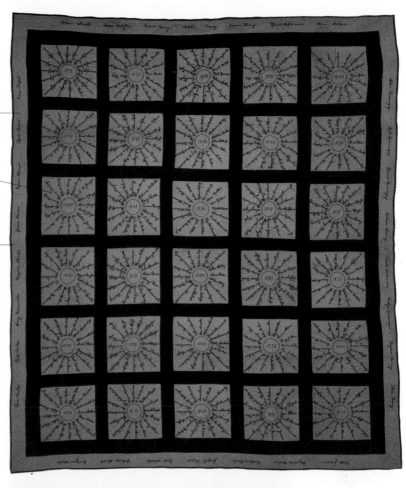

◄ In this cotton quilt, the amount of the donation is written in the center of each block. The amounts range from $1.10 to $25.05. Since these were large sums of money at the time that the quilt was made, we can assume that it was a Fundraiser for an especially important cause and/or sponsored by a well-to-do community. Unfortunately, there is no reference to the purpose for which the quilt was made.

▲ Red and white are the colors seen most often in Fundraising quilts. The solid red grid gives this version more visual punch than many similar examples in which the embroidery provides the only pattern.

◄ In this example, the wheel pattern is created solely from the embroidered names. Other variations were pieced wheels with names written in ink or embroidered between the spokes.

Charm Quilts

A Charm quilt is distinguished by its component fabrics each being used only a single time. The quilt may be made in any pattern, but the defining characteristic is that no fabric is repeated within it.

The term "Charm quilt" is linked to the fashion for collecting one-of-a-kind buttons, popular from the 1850s through the 1870s. It was customary for a young woman to string her buttons together on a "charm string" in hopes that her Prince Charming would arrive before she collected 1,000 buttons.

In the 19th century, Charm quilts were also known as "beggar's quilts," because a maker often got her material by begging it from others. Women traded fabrics and used mill samples to broaden their inventories. By the 20th century, however, fabric companies offered packages of material geared toward Charm quilt makers.

Most Charm quilt patterns use hexagonal blocks. When designed effectively, the combination of fabrics creates the illusion of stars and/or tumbling blocks, triangles, or diamond shapes. It often takes close examination to recognize a Charm quilt: the chosen fabrics may be so similar in color and pattern that the viewer must see pieces side by side to distinguish their differences. Most of Charm fabrics are prints, but solids may also be incorporated.

Although popular in the third quarter of the 19th century, Charm quilts declined by the beginning of the 20th century. Revivals occurred during the 1920s and 1930s and from the 1970s until the present. The price of Charm quilts varies greatly. The value of an individual example is determined primarily by the intricacy and beauty of its pattern and by its condition.

Star-Pattern Quilt, Lancaster, Pennsylvania, c.1880

The subtle use of multiple patterns enhances the appeal and value of this quilt.

The unusual stars in this quilt are all six-pointed rather than the more commonly seen eight-pointed design.

The pristine, unwashed condition of this quilt greatly increases its value.

The use of solid colors only in the central star provides visual focus in the center, from which the overall design radiates— another indication of the quilt maker's strong sense of design.

The darker outline around the central star creates a herringbone effect in addition to highlighting the star itself.

The interplay of patterns is continued by the lighter brown stars in each corner, which can also be seen as tumbling blocks.

Size: 80 x 91in/
2.03 x 2.31m
Value: $3,000–$4,000

Zigzag Border Quilt, Lancaster County, *c.*1880s

Corner blocks were made of pinwheels.

The zigzag border provides a nice frame for the quilt.

The distribution of color leads the eye throughout the quilt, rather than to any particular focal point.

The colors of the border reflect a regional taste, particular to this area of rural Pennsylvania.

Although the arrangement of darks and lights is well done here, the design forms neither an overall pattern nor individual patterns, making this piece less valuable than the example opposite.

Size: 84 x 94in/
2.08 x 2.38m
Value: $700–$1,200

◀ *This quilt was created entirely of diamond-shaped cotton pieces, which were continued to form the border. Solid colors were used only for the central star; elsewhere, the fabrics are prints. There are many patterns within the quilt in addition to the overall pattern.*

▲ *This cotton quilt consists of elongated hexagonal elements with a zigzag-pattern border.*

◀ *Charm quilts can be difficult to recognize, because some of the component pieces may resemble one another closely. This similarity of fabrics often gives a more unified appearance than one would expect from the use of several hundred fabrics in a single quilt. Here, the individual hexagonal elements are diverse in color and pattern but combine harmoniously.*

Crib Quilts

When a young woman became engaged to marry, she was expected to have 12 quilts. The thirteenth was her bridal quilt. She would make more quilts as her family grew. Crib quilts, though, celebrated the birth of specific children. These works of art, because of their size, rarity, individuality, and loving connotations make them highly desirable to collectors.

Crib quilts are generally square rather than rectangular and 36in/91.4cm across, although examples with variations up to 12in/30.5cm in either direction may be found. Price is not proportional to size. Because of their rarity, genuine Crib quilts compare in price to full-size quilts of similar quality. Many fewer Crib quilts were made, and fewer have survived because of hard use and many washings.

Some skepticism is needed to evaluate a Crib quilt's integrity. The prices these diminutive bedcovers fetch have generated many knockoff "Crib quilts." A full-size bedcover can be reduced to as many as four bogus crib-size quilts; a damaged quilt may yield one or two. Large-scale blocks may reveal a fake. A true miniature with propotionally small blocks is most desirable. Ideally, a Crib quilt has a border. In addition to providing visual interest, a border indicates that a quilt is not a rebound fragment. Not all genuine Crib quilts, though, were made with borders. For this reason, it is important to pay particular attention to the binding. It should be made from fabric that is consistent with the age of the quilt and appropriate to the rest of the piece.

Diamond-Pattern Crib Quilt, Pennsylvania, c.1890

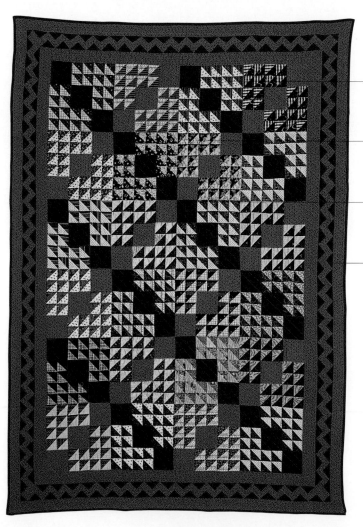

The blocks filled with triangles draw the eye in and around in a swirling motion.

The triangle motif can be seen as a variation on Ocean Waves (see page 126–127).

The red and yellow four-patches look as though they are superimposed on the triangles.

The zigzag border introduces a new shape that complements the interior forms.

Size: 40 x 6oin/
1.02 x 1.55m
Value $2,000–$3,000

Basket-Pattern Crib Quilt, Pennsylvania, c.1900

The border's intersections on the ends form unusual corner blocks.

The vine and leaf border is a charming attempt to replicate the type of pattern seen more often in finer quilts.

Sashing between the baskets forms a zigzag pattern that is very striking.

The baskets and their handles, in particular, are crudely made. The handles are irregular and inconsistent in shape and size, and the bases are too small.

Incorporating half-stars on top and the "T" on the bottom is an imaginative use of the space.

Size: 31 x 44in/
0.79 x 1.12m
Value: $800–$1,600

▸ *The concept and design of this cotton quilt are better than the implementation. Although not finely made, this was, without doubt, always a Crib quilt. The size and placement of the blocks, as well as the presence of the border, indicate that this was not cut down from a larger quilt. (The same factors apply to the example on the opposite page.)*

◂ *This cotton quilt was made in Lehigh County, Penn. This is an original, complex combination of patterns. The color choices and the diagonal setting contribute to a sense of depth and movement.*

A View of Children

Throughout most of the 19th century, children were viewed as miniature adults. It is logical, then, that children's quilts would be miniatures of traditional full-size quilts and not original, child-oriented designs.

This view of children began to change during Victorian times. In 1912, the famed quilt designer Marie Webster *(see page 93)* created one of the first patterns for a small quilt with a juvenile theme. Her designs were immediately popular and sold well throughout the 1940s. Most figural Crib quilts—quilts with recognizable pictures of people, animals, and amusements—especially those done in solid color pastels, are kit patterns from the early 20th century.

▴ *This enchanting Crib quilt (35 x 48in/0.89 x 1.23m) depicting children watching a marionette show was made in Pennsylvania, c.1930.*

Doll Quilts

Many Doll quilts were made as practice pieces by young girls, some as young as 3, who were learning to sew. It is possible to find Doll quilts that use complex patterns and display fine quilting, but more often, they are simple, pieced quilts made from basic patterns. Because of their relative simplicity and straight seams, four-patch and nine-patch patterns were popular choices for beginners, and many Doll quilts use these patterns. A rare few examples are appliquéd.

Quite a number of Doll quilts were quilted by machine, even if pieced by hand. (It is easy to imagine a busy mother devoting only so much time to creating a bedcover for her daughter's toy.) Whether a Doll quilt is stitched by hand or machine has little bearing on its value. The pattern, color, and scale are far more important, as is the assurance that the piece was not cut down from something larger. As with Crib quilts, the demand for these appealing miniatures has led to some unscrupulous practices *(see page 72).*

The same criteria for evaluating Crib quilts apply to Doll quilts. Check that the fabrics, workmanship, and overall condition of the quilt are consistent. In particular, the binding or border may seem "off" if the quilt was cut from a larger piece. Miniaturization of scale is even more important here than in Crib quilts and gives successful renditions an irresistible charm. Because Doll quilts were often practice pieces created by children, collectors are more forgiving of crude quilting and the use of basic patterns in these pieces. For many, these imperfections make the quilts even more dear.

Four Patch Doll Quilt, New England, *c.*1850

The scale of the blocks and the presence of the border confirm that this was made for a doll.

Though the pattern is simple, some of the fabrics, particularly the border print, are quite elegant.

The piece is quilted by hand with more detail than is seen on most Doll quilts.

Size: 20 x 21in/
51m x 53cm
Value: $400–$800

Flying Geese Doll Quilt, Pennsylvania, c.1880

The Flying Geese pattern is unusual. Angled pieces are harder to sew, even for more experienced quilters.

This example was quilted by machine but interestingly, bound by hand.

Both the small-scale triangles and the binding indicate that this piece was not cut down.

Size: 10 x 14in/
25.4 x 35.5cm
Value: $200–$300

▶ *The addition of a border would have made this cotton quilt a more desirable piece. It would have provided both a more finished appearance and further assurance of the quilt's integrity.*

◀ *The four-patch pattern in this cotton quilt is typical of the practice pieces made by young sewers. The elegant fabrics and the relatively fine workmanship indicate, however, that it was probably made by an adult.*

Starting Out

No other quilt could better illustrate that crude piecing and machine quilting can be charming in a doll-size quilt. This was undoubtedly a practice piece done by a child—perhaps her first attempt. We would cringe at the sight of this had it been done as a full-size quilt. Knowing a young girl created it makes the poor craftsmanship more than forgivable.

▶ *This cotton Doll quilt, c.1940, was made in Western Pennsylvania and is of Amish origin. The quilt is a true miniature, 9 x 12in/22.8 x 30.5cm, of the pattern known as Hole in the Barn.*

Lancaster Amish Diamonds

Lancaster County, Penn., is home to one of the oldest and largest Amish communities in the United States. The quilts made by the Lancaster County Amish are among the most distinctive—and strikingly contemporary in appearance—of all antique quilts. Characterized by sophisticated juxtaposition of solid colors, bold geometry, and exquisite quilting, these quilts were usually limited to three patterns—Center Diamond, Bars *(see page 78)*, and Sunshine and Shadow *(see box)*—but the variations within the limitation can be staggering.

The aesthetic that guides these quilts is rooted in the religious and communal beliefs of the Amish. This group fled religious persecution in Europe and settled in what is now Pennsylvania throughout the 18th century. Dedicated to a simple, devout life with minimal influence from the "outside world," they govern their daily lives by a strict and literal adherence to the Christian Bible and sets of guidelines regarding such things as clothing, styles of houses and their decoration, and the adoption or rejection

of technology. These guidelines vary somewhat from community to community, but any newcomers are expected to follow them. In order to demonstrate their submission to God's authority, the Amish embrace a manner that is modest, calm, and quiet—which makes the vibrancy of their quilts all the more striking.

The best-known Lancaster County pattern is the Center Diamond. The Amish did not begin making quilts in this pattern, based on the Center Medallion quilts popular in mid-19th century, until nearly the end of the century. Lancaster Amish quilts share other distinctive features: they are square, have wide borders and bindings, and often include corner blocks. Almost all of the tops were pieced on foot-pedal-powered sewing machines, and the bindings were at least partly applied by machine. The often-lavish quilting was always done by hand. Only solid-color fabrics appear on the quilt top, but there may be small patterning on the backing. The Amish used patterns other than those mentioned, but such quilts are atypical.

Lancaster Amish Diamond, Pennsylvania, c.1915

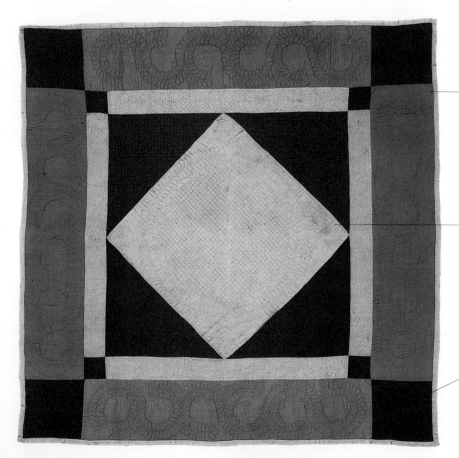

The deep feathers in the mauve border and the pumpkin seeds quilted in the inner border are desirable patterns typical of early examples.

Most of the quilting in the diamond is a basic waffle, or crosshatch, pattern. This is not as ornamental as the quilting in the finest examples.

The use of corner blocks in this quilt anchors the pattern (as compared to the example opposite, where the diamond seems to float).

Size: 88in/2.23m square
Value: $3,000–$5,000

Lancaster Amish Floating Diamond, Pennsylvania, *c.*1915

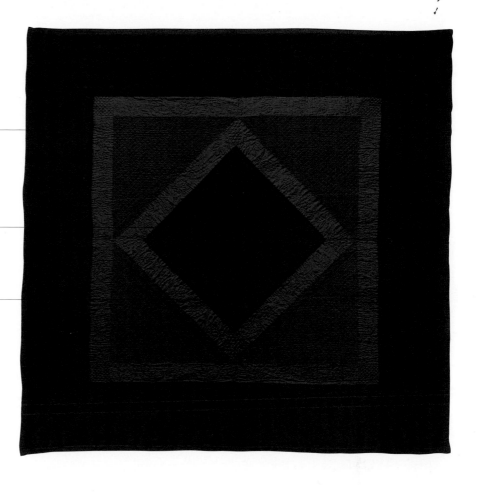

The consistent use of saturated, jewellike colors makes this quilt especially desirable.

Many feel that red is the preferred color for the central diamond. The use of it in this quilt would certainly support that belief.

The fine quilting, particularly in the center, adds beautiful texture.

Size: 84in/2.13m square
Value: $10,000+

▶*When this pattern is made without corner blocks, as it is in this woolen quilt, it is called Floating Diamond. The effect is enhanced in this example by the choice of color.*

◀ *The major drawback of this woolen quilt is the unevenness of color. Particularly in the central diamond, it is distracting to the eye.*

Sunshine and Shadow

The Sunshine and Shadow pattern is composed of a single patch—a small square—repeated in concentric, diamond-shaped rows in graduated light and dark colors. In the best examples, the lights and darks are deftly arranged to create visual movement; they seem to shimmer outward from the center. Although established much earlier, this pattern appeared most often in later examples. The name Sunshine and Shadow is used interchangeably with Trip Around the World. In both patterns, blocks can be set either square or on-point.

Lancaster Amish Bars

The Amish quilters of Lancaster County have transformed several simple geometric patterns into brilliant works of art. Curiously, the Amish regarded piecing not as an admirable expression of thrift, but rather as "worldly"—a prohibitive criticism. Their quilts, therefore, were made of wide bands and fields of fabric that were purchased specifically for bedcovers. Few simpler patterns exist than those of the Bars and Diamond quilts. Yet they incorporate rich colors as sweeping backdrops to some of the most dazzling quilting ever seen.

Color and quilting are the main criteria of excellence for a collector when evaluating an Amish quilt. The borders are often embellished with feathered vines or scrolls, and the central diamond is filled with concentric stars or wreaths—all curved designs that testify to great skill on the quilter's part. Botanical imagery often appears and can help establish the date of the quilt. Vines, wreaths, grapes, and pumpkin seeds predominated in early examples; quilted roses indicate a later piece.

Diamonds appeared in greater numbers than Bars. Later quilts often display the Sunshine and Shadow pattern. More rare were versions of other patterns such as Nine Patch *(see page 100)*, Double Nine Patch, Irish Chain *(see page 114)*, and Crazy quilts *(see pages 60–63)*. All of the variations can be identified as Amish by their fabrics, quilting patterns, and overall structure.

The heyday of Lancaster Amish quilts lasted from 1900 to 1930. In the 1930s, both quilting patterns and fabrics began to change. Early examples of Amish quilts were made of fine woolen fabrics; later examples are flat rayon, rayon crepe, or blends of rayon and wool. Few were made of cotton; 1950s quilts may include polyester.

Early woolen Lancaster Amish quilts are extremely desirable to collectors. A relatively small group made these quilts during a fairly short period of time, so demand can outstrip supply. Most prime examples sell for upwards of $10,000. A quilt made after 1940 with synthetic fabrics generally sells in the low thousands.

Lancaster Amish Bars Quilt, Pennsylvania, *c.*1930

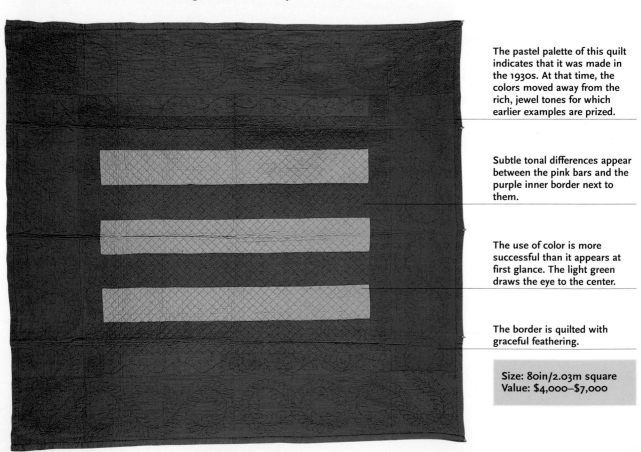

The pastel palette of this quilt indicates that it was made in the 1930s. At that time, the colors moved away from the rich, jewel tones for which earlier examples are prized.

Subtle tonal differences appear between the pink bars and the purple inner border next to them.

The use of color is more successful than it appears at first glance. The light green draws the eye to the center.

The border is quilted with graceful feathering.

Size: 80in/2.03m square
Value: $4,000–$7,000

Lancaster Amish Split Bars Quilt, Pennsylvania, *c.*1915

The colors are the traditional, intense shades that are most sought by collectors.

This example is even more out of the ordinary than the example opposite because the quilter split the bars and used deeper blue in the center bars.

The quilter used a crosshatch pattern for the interior quilting.

Size: 84in/2.13m square
Value: $12,000+

◄ Notice the difference between hanging the Bars pattern vertically and hanging it horizontally. Each produces a striking but different effect.

▲ This is a more complex variation than typical of the standard Bars. Usually, each bar is the same width. In Split Bars, such as this, the quilt maker divides alternate rows.

◄ Although made far less often than Diamonds and Bars, the Double Nine Patch quilt is one of the established patterns made by the Lancaster County Amish. The blocks were either set square, as seen in this example, or on point.

Hawaiian Appliqué Quilts

issionaries from New England arrived in Hawaii
in 1820. As part of their effort to persuade the
Hawaiians to be more like them, missionary
women immediately invited royal Hawaiians to join their
sewing circles. There, they introduced the natives to their
fabrics, sewing, and quilting techniques. The traditional
Hawaiian fabric, called kapa, was made from the bark of
mulberry trees. To make a patterned bedcover or wall
hanging, one batch of the kapa was dyed, then pounded
into a background fabric with a mallet. The practices of
the Hawaiians and the traditions of the missionaries
merged toward the end of the 19th century, giving birth to
the elaborate format now known as Hawaiian Appliqué.

A typical Hawaiian Appliqué quilt consists of one large
appliqué pattern cut from a single piece of folded cloth.
Both the appliqué and the background fabric are solid
colors; usually the ground is white and the appliqué is a
strong contrasting color, such as red or navy blue. These
quilts also feature an idiosyncratic form of quilting, called
"echo" quilting, in which the stitching follows the outline
of the appliqué, radiating out in concentric, parallel lines.

Bold, two-color quilts from Pennsylvania are sometimes
mistaken for Hawaiian quilts, but in fact, they usually can
be distinguished by their quilting patterns. Those from the
mainland are rarely finished with echo quilting.

Hawaiian quilt makers took their inspiration from
nature. The shapes of their appliqués are stylized
interpretations of Hawaiian plants and animals, such as
ferns, lilies, hibiscus, breadfruit, pineapples, and turtles. The
patterns belonged to specific makers or families and had
symbolic meanings, so quilters did not trade patterns.

Another distinctive quilt, called *My Beloved Flag* or *Lost
Beloved Flag*, is also exclusively Hawaiian. In 1893, the
Hawaiian Islands became a United States territory. The
queen abdicated her throne and the royal Hawaiian flag
was lowered. For a short time, native quilt makers
expressed their patriotism in quilts that had combinations
of the crown, the Royal Coat of Arms, and the images on
the Hawaiian flag—the Union Jack and eight red, white,
and blue stripes that represent the main Hawaiian islands.

Examples of both traditional appliqué and "Flag" quilts
are extremely rare and highly prized by collectors.

Appliqué Quilt, Hawaii, *c.*1880

The appliqué pattern is
extremely intricate. It utilizes
both appliqué and reverse
appliqué work.

The echo quilting around the
appliqué is also very elaborately
done.

The red binding provides a
minimal frame. This type of
quilt is rarely made with a
patterned border.

Size: 77in/1.96m square
Value: $5,000–$7,000

"My Beloved Flag" Quilt, Hawaii, *c.*1900

Although portions resemble the British Union Jack, this is actually four Hawaiian flags.

The center form represents the Hawaiian crown, which was retired when the queen abdicated. Some versions include an appliqué of the word "aloha" instead of, or in addition to, the crown.

Some echo quilting occurs around the central appliqués.

Most of the quilting is done in straight lines, with moderate-size stitches.

Size: 84in/2.13m square
Value: $8,000–$12,000

▶ *This style of quilt is slightly rarer than the example opposite, which makes it more valuable. The quilts were made for a fairly brief period following the lowering of the Hawaiian flag in 1893. So few of these quilts come on the market that collectors will often accept them in compromised condition. This example, however, is in excellent condition.*

◀ *Appliqué quilts of this type were made in Hawaii from the late 19th century through the present. Both this quilt and the one above are fine examples of Hawaiian quilts; the value difference is somewhat arbitrary and might in fact disappear, depending on the preferences of the buyer.*

Creating a Hawaiian Appliqué

The large, ornate, single appliqué patterns that distinguish Hawaiian Appliqué quilts are made by creating paper patterns similar to the popular "snowflakes" made of cut paper. The quilt maker folds a large square in half to form a rectangle, then folds down the rectangle to form a square. Finally, the square is folded diagonally to form a triangle. The design is drawn on the folded edges and carefully cut out. Some portion of the folded edge must remain intact so that when the paper is unfolded, it forms one perfectly symmetrical, four-part motif.

The Hawaiian motifs vary from literal representations, such as flowers or ferns, to geometric and abstract shapes that resemble snowflakes. In whatever form, these designs create a balanced and pleasing effect. The quilts are usually square, with the appliqués covering most of the surface.

Variations in the basic design have appeared in more recent times. Contemporary quilters sometimes add corner motifs or a scalloped border (called a "lei"). They also may use more than one color or add printed fabrics to traditional patterns.

Though attractive, modern examples with these innovations have two strikes against them: they lack the rarity of unusual early examples, and they lack the age that draws collectors to the antique market.

Pictorial Quilts

The technical term for quilts with realistic representations of people, animals, objects, or scenes is Pictorial. The earliest examples appeared in the late 18th century, but they are a rarity from any era. Pictorial quilts have their roots in European needlework traditions, particularly tapestry and embroidery, that used symbolic imagery to relate stories or convey messages to people who could not read.

In the United States, the tradition carried over to Pictorial quilts of different types. In some forms, the message of the quilt's pictures was relatively simple, with a single theme in view. Pineapples, for example, symbolized hospitality, and red roses denoted true love. Hearts indicated love and marriage—and were not used frivolously. A young woman was thought to jeopardize her prospects for marriage if she made a quilt with heart images before she was engaged.

Some Pictorial quilts tell stories that we can decipher as we would the images in a painting. Like a painting, the images may suggest more than one interpretation. Others depict landscapes or urban scenes, or commemorate specific events *(see page 45)*.

Pictorial quilts appeared in the block style and as Center Medallions, and they are almost always appliqué. Examples from the 18th and 19th centuries show clear signs that they were unique and completely original; the quilt makers had no purchased patterns to rely upon and did not trade designs among themselves.

Patterns did become commercially available in the 20th century, and a few small companies that made them, such as Story Book Quilts, thrived. But from the standpoint of collecting, the use of a commercial pattern constitutes a shortcoming. Such quilts resemble Kit quilts in that they allowed virtually any needlewoman to tell a story, albeit the same story, in fabric. However charming the end result, the quilt does not reflect the quilter's unique life experience, making these examples of less interest to collectors. The most desirable Pictorial quilts relate stories or experiences that are particular to the makers.

"The Asylum" Quilt, Catonsville, Maryland, *c.*1850

The appliqué depicts black and white people who appear unhappy, and, in some cases, in conflict with one another. Their clothing and facial expressions are rendered in unusual detail.

Flowers, birds, animals, snakes, and other reptiles are repeated throughout the quilt. Their specific meanings are not known, but they add to the impression that the maker was conveying a story she found painful.

This quilt is imaginative and finely crafted, and it exemplifies the importance Pictorial quilts have played in people's lives.

Size: 79 x 89in/
2 x 2.26m
Value: $150,000+

Little Women Quilt, New York City, *c.*1945

The appliqué figures are shown in great detail.

This example is the only known example in which the alternate block is a printed patchwork.

The triangles are not pieced; they are made of cheater's cloth (*see page 141*).

The quilting was secondary to the appliqué and was never more than a basic geometric pattern.

Size: 86 x 100in/
2.18 x 2.54 m
Value: $1,500–$2,500

▶ *Made by Marion Cheever Whiteside Newton's Story Book Quilts, this cotton quilt is the standard format for Mrs. Newton's Pictorial quilts. They vary in size, but each one consists of an appliqué block alternating with a plain block. No Story Book quilt has a border.*

◀ *Oral history relates that a young woman who was hospitalized at Spring Grove State Hospital made this cotton quilt during her stay at the facility. Little more is known of her life than that she was admitted while pregnant out of wedlock, and she died at the asylum. The meanings of the images cannot readily be deciphered, yet the viewer cannot help but be affected by the images. The quilt maker has certainly conveyed her sense of struggle. It seems a shame that her meaning cannot be understood more clearly. At the same time, the ambiguity adds to the fascination the quilt engenders.*

The Story Book Quilt Company

Founded in 1940 by Marion Cheever Whiteside Newton, Story Book Quilts sold designs that she had created either as patterns, kits to be assembled, or completed quilts. Mrs. Newton made appliqués for stories such as *Little Women* and *Alice in Wonderland*, eventually establishing an inventory of 50 pictorial patterns.

Not all her themes were geared toward children, however. She also created a series relating to horses, in which she included patterns called "Polo" and "The Fox Hunt." Another of her series depicts a variety of military uniforms.

Mrs. Newton's appliqué blocks related stories in great detail and were drawn with painstaking care. She researched each subject and provided specific and extraordinary historical accuracy in her depictions of clothing and events. Technically, her quilts are so expert that one found a place in the textile collection of the Metropolitan Museum of Art in New York City. Their only shortcoming for some collectors, if one considers it so, is that the designs were commercially designed and distributed, rather than created solely as an expression of a particular quilt maker's imagination.

Eccentric Quilts

Quilts in this category are defined by what they are not—identifiable examples of a certain style or pattern. These quilts ignore most of the accepted guidelines for what constitutes a desirable quilt. Quilting stitches, when any exist, are barely distinguishable from basting stitches and are blithely referred to as "toenail catchers." Many examples of Eccentric quilts are tied rather than quilted. Any piecing or appliqué tends to be crude and the fabrics inexpensive. Why would anyone want such a quilt? Because whatever they may lack in technique, they more than make up for in innovative color and design. Eccentric quilts are imaginative and unpredictable in ways that more conventional quilts are not.

Eccentric quilts are often made from bits of fabric that cost little, and this suggests that the makers may have been poor. Many of these quilts originated in rural areas, where the makers were almost certainly isolated from the work of other quilters. Although rarely well sewn, many of the quilts are finished works that rival those of fine artists. The composition, design, and colors can combine to form an unusual, unexpected, and pleasing whole. Whether the makers thought in terms of making art or were simply making functional bedcovers, modern collectors interpret the Eccentric quilt as outsider art.

As with any work of art, evaluation of Eccentric quilts is subjective. The standard benchmarks of quilt quality—needlework, craftsmanship, and fabrics—do not apply. Eccentrics fail all the tests. Yet as artistic expressions, they can fare very well. Certainly not every crudely made quilt should be renamed art, but poor technique alone does not disqualify a quilt from being desirable. Eccentric quilts demand evaluation on their own terms.

Eccentric quilts have the potential to provide a buyer with unique artwork at minimal cost. While gaining in popularity, these quilts are still largely underappreciated and undervalued. If a buyer is prepared to suspend conventional criteria, such a quilt may offer a pleasant surprise and a hidden treasure.

Abstract Quilt, Pennsylvania, c.1900

The maker of this quilt created a dynamic abstract composition that can successfully be viewed and appreciated either vertically or horizontally.

The cable quilting used here is better than on most examples of this type. It contributes to the rich texture of the nubby wools used to make the quilt.

Light and dark are well distributed, further enhancing the visual interest of the quilt.

Size: 72 x 86in/
1.83 x 2.18
Value: $2,000–$3,000

Strip Quilt, York County, Pennsylvania, *c.*1930

This is essentially a Strip quilt. The four bars are filled with a combination of patterns probably never assembled in any other quilt.

The materials are appliqued to a muslin ground.

It is literally a fabric collage. The quilt maker assembled fabrics that range from fancy glazed chintz to the printed labels of feedsacks.

While the pattern and colors create an interesting composition, they do not achieve the energy of the example opposite. It is certainly not a fine quilt.

Size: 68 x 77in
1.73 x 1.95m
Value: $800–$1,200

It would be fascinating to know why the maker of this woolen quilt went from very large blocks of fabric to miniscule pieces. Did she use the tiny cuttings as an artist would dabs of color? Or was she thriftily using fabric scraps she had on hand to fill small spaces? The collector can only speculate.

This example has many of the characteristics often attributed to African-American quilts (see page 84), and it would be easy enough to mistakenly assign it to that category of work. In fact, this quilter was Caucasian. As always, even educated guesswork cannot substitute for provenance in determining the history and value of an antique quilt.

The quilt incorporates hints of traditional patterns with totally unorthodox patterning.

Novelty Quilts

Quilts are described as Novelties in two cases: when the material of which they were constructed is something other than typical yard goods such as wool, cotton, silk, or velvet; or if the subject depicted is unusual. To some degree, every quilt made by hand is a unique item. Novelty quilts, however, are defined by their individuality; they fall into the Novelty category simply by being difficult to categorize.

In the late 19th century, cigar bands and tobacco pouch labels were made from silk, usually yellow strips with black printing. Numerous Novelty quilts and cushion covers were made from them. In the early 20th century, cigarette companies offered printed flannel flags of different nations as premiums with their product. These were combined to create Novelty quilt tops that were either tied or quilted. A late 20th-century quilt made of plastic bread wrappers is one of the more spectacularly unusual Novelty quilts that can be found today.

Quilts that illustrate out-of-the-ordinary subject matter are also considered Novelties. A small number of these picture, for instance, U.S. maps or specific states. Without published or widely used patterns, no two are the same. Quilts made for specific events may be Novelties. For example, Sears, Roebuck, and Company sponsored a contest for the nation's best quilt maker at the 1933 Chicago World's Fair, offering a special prize for a quilt made to honor the fair's theme: A Century of Progress. A staggering 25,000 quilts were submitted. Any of these with original designs would qualify as a Novelty quilt. In the late 20th century, no better example exists than the AIDS memorial quilt. Concept and individual panels are unique.

When evaluating a Novelty quilt, it is wise not to be too literal. Overlap often exists between the Novelty quilt and quilts of other categories. Place more emphasis on the image, the workmanship, the design, and the intent of the maker than on the category.

Suede Leather Quilt, Maryland, c.1950

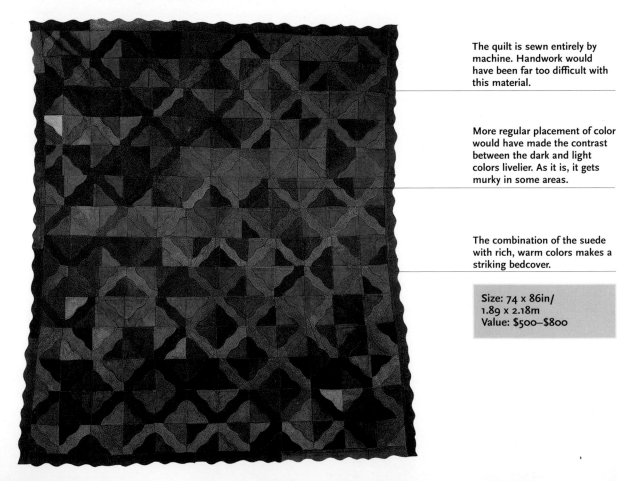

The quilt is sewn entirely by machine. Handwork would have been far too difficult with this material.

More regular placement of color would have made the contrast between the dark and light colors livelier. As it is, it gets murky in some areas.

The combination of the suede with rich, warm colors makes a striking bedcover.

Size: 74 x 86in/
1.89 x 2.18m
Value: $500–$800

Cartoon Character Quilt, Pennsylvania, *c.*1930

The Walt Disney characters in the embroidered vignettes are seen in quilts even less frequently than Mickey and Minnie Mouse.

This quilt is expertly crafted. Many details are included that add to the quilt's appeal.

The billowing skirts make the Minnies look like three-dimensional dolls that could be lifted out of the quilt and held.

The embroidered scenes are quite amusing and would bring a smile to the face of any child or adult.

Size: 67 x 84in/
1.70 x 2.13m
Value: $15,000+

◀ *A variation of the pattern* **Robbing Peter to Pay Paul** *(see page 162), this quilt is considered a Novelty because of the material from which it is made. Very few quilts of any type were made of suede leather.*

▲ *This cotton quilt qualifies as a Novelty because of the subject matter. Given their popularity, it is surprising how rarely Mickey and Minnie Mouse served as the subjects of quilts.*

◀ *The combination of appliqué and embroidered figures here is quite unusual. Both types are extremely well executed in this quilt.*

Kit Quilts

Kit quilts were the fabric equivalents of paint-by-numbers artwork. Almost regardless of needlework skill, quilters were able to purchase and assemble patterns and components for quilts that were often delicate and quite pretty.

Kits came in several different types: pre-cut pieces to be assembled; basted quilts to be completed; or finished products. Kit quilts were sold in the 1920s and 1930s in response to the Colonial Revival home-decorating movement. Pattern makers tended to romanticize earlier times and appealed to their customers' sense of nostalgia. Quilts were marked with names like Betsy Ross Tulip Bed or Grandma Dexter Quilt Blocks.

In reality, 19th-century quilts reflected the styles and tastes of the communities in which they were made. Kit quilts lacked the individuality and "personality" of these earlier quilts in exchange for nationwide homogeneity.

Most Kit quilts were composed of solid-color, pastel fabrics. The motifs were usually floral, often in a center-medallion format with a great deal of plain background. Many were finished with scalloped edges. Unlike the stylized floral patterns of the 19th century, Kit quilts offered literal images of flowers. The pre-cut pieces included fabrics in a range of colors varied enough to convey shading in leaves and flowers. Additional detail was provided with embroidery. One of the clues to identifying a Kit quilt is visible evidence of the preprinted blue lines that indicated to the maker where the piece was supposed to be stitched.

In the late 20th century, kit quilts have been very popular with those looking for soft, pleasing colors with which to decorate their homes. Serious collectors seek more imaginative quilts, but one cannot overlook the fresh, often springlike qualities of most kit quilts.

"French Basket" Pattern, origin unknown, c.1930

The original signature and date (Agneta Voss Petersen, 1930) are relatively rare features in Kit quilts.

Each element of this pattern is unusually graceful and complex.

The use of pink and green with the yellow centers to the flowers provides a lovely counterpoint to the overall blue and white.

This is among the most sought-after of Marie Webster patterns, examples of which are rarely seen.

The twisted basket handles are echoed by the blue loops in the alternate blocks. This is a subtle and successful design element.

The placement of the baskets on crisscross diagonals adds even more to the unity and unusual sophistication of this overall design.

Size: 84in/2.13m square
Value: $1,000–$2,000

Lattice Basket Quilt, Pennsylvania, *c.*1930

The scalloped edge adds grace to the pattern, which is otherwise relatively simple.

The attempt at the undulating ribbon with corner bows is attractive, but the quality of the sewing detracts from value.

While the use of hearts in the quilting is a nice feature, the quilting is not well done: the stitches are fairly large and far apart.

There is a great deal of white space, a common characteristic of kit quilts. In this instance, more detail in the pattern would have made a more luxuriant quilt.

Size: 78 x 86 in/
1.98 x 2.18m)
Value: $500–$900

▶ *The pattern for this cotton quilt was available nationwide. Using solid-color fabrics, the quilt was made in a center-medallion format. Heart-shaped quilting surrounds the central basket and each of the flowers outside the ribbon frame.*

◀ *Designed by Marie Webster in 1914, this cotton quilt is composed entirely of solid-color fabrics. Feather-pattern quilting was used in the border, while the blue areas show diagonal stitching lines, and the white centers are quilted with wreaths.*

The Queen of Kits

Marie Webster was the undisputed leader of the quilt revival movement of the 20th century. Born in Indiana in 1859, Webster was raised in a wealthy family and traveled throughout the United States and Europe, where she was exposed to the Art Nouveau movement. This aesthetic emphasized close observation of and unity with nature, manifest in the use of delicate, curvilinear forms.

Webster made her first appliqué quilt in 1909, at the age of 50. She was an avid gardener and created patterns featuring delicate, naturalistic flowers.

Her designs represented a radical shift from the bold red-and-green stylized floral designs of the late 19th century.

Webster's designs were first published in the *Ladies' Home Journal* in 1911. In all, she created 33 original patterns. Demand for them became so great that she formed the Practical Patchwork Company in 1920—the very first Kit-quilt company. She also wrote the first book about quilts published in the United States. *Quilts: Their Story and How to Make Them* appeared in 1915 and remains an important reference to this day.

Embroidered Quilts

American quilts have been embellished with embroidery since the 18th century, but not until the last quarter of the 19th century did embroidery provide the sole design motifs. Embroidered quilts arose from the fashion for art needlework *(see page 64)* and paralleled the use of embroidery in Victorian Crazy quilts *(see page 60)*. They were typically made of cotton. While many were quilted, probably an equal number served as summer spreads, and therefore have a backing but no batting; this eliminates the quilting needed to keep the batting from shifting. On quilted examples, the stitching is rarely elaborate. The embroidery itself was done in a simple overlapping stitch, called a stem stitch. The quilt maker sewed only the outline of the image and did not fill in the pictures. The greatest number of Embroidered quilts appeared in red-on-white, with blue-on-white a distant second. Only beginning in the 1920s did multiple colors enter into use. The blocks were set with or without sashing. Where sashing exists, it often has an embroidered grid.

The fad for Embroidered quilts lasted from the 1880s until the 1930s, and the motifs used offer the collector hints as to when a quilt was made. The earliest examples used the same motifs as Victorian Crazy quilts: owls, Japanese fans, butterflies, and insects. Images of silverware and china became popular early in the 20th century. Quilt makers also incorporated souvenir blocks known as "penny squares," available for sale at the Pan-American Exposition in 1901. While many of these depicted public buildings, the best known image is of President William McKinley (who tragicall, was assassinated while attending the Exposition). Quilters availed themselves of blocks created to commemorate special events, such as elections or the entry of a new state into the Union. Beginning in the 1920s, quilters used blocks with such themes as days of the week or state birds. Not all Embroidered quilts featured commercial blocks. Individuals created squares with themes of importance to them, and religious groups often embroidered large images of their church as the center blocks on their Fundraising quilts *(see page 68)*.

Until recently, Embroidered quilts were of little interest to collectors. In the last few years, prices for interesting examples have begun to rise.

Victorian Quilt, Pennsylvania, *c.*1915

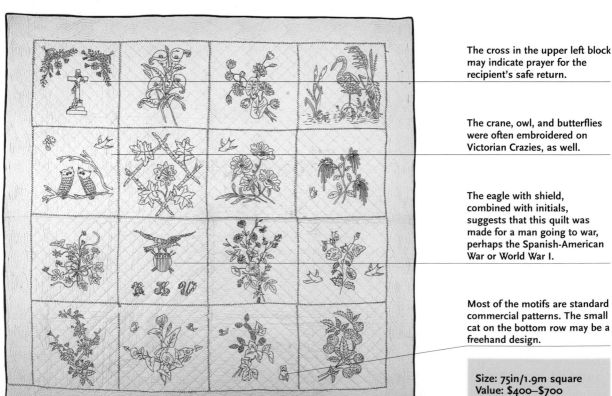

The cross in the upper left block may indicate prayer for the recipient's safe return.

The crane, owl, and butterflies were often embroidered on Victorian Crazies, as well.

The eagle with shield, combined with initials, suggests that this quilt was made for a man going to war, perhaps the Spanish-American War or World War I.

Most of the motifs are standard commercial patterns. The small cat on the bottom row may be a freehand design.

Size: 75in/1.9m square
Value: $400–$700

Juvenile Quilt, Pennsylvania, dated 1930 and initialed MAO

Repetition of the horseshoe in the center and four corners adds unity to the composition.

The quilting is finer than that usually done on Embroidered quilts.

Many, but not all, of the designs are commercial patterns.

The quilt is made livelier by the use of multicolor embroidery.

Size: 70 x 73in/
1.78 x 1.85m
Value: $600–$900

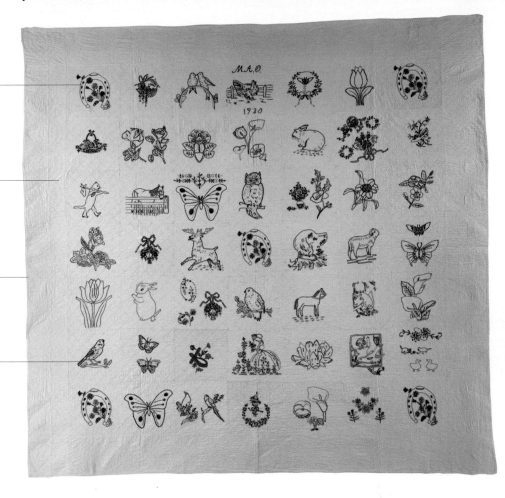

◀ *Many of the motifs used on this cotton quilt recall those on Victorian Crazy quilts (see page 60), indicating the likelihood of a relatively early date of creataion. This example does not have any of the juvenile patterns often found in embroidered quilts.*

▶ *The two blocks shown here, illustrating the Puss in Boots and the horse, are particularly charming and almost certainly homemade.*

▲ *This cotton quilt was clearly made for a child— most of the motifs are juvenile and cheerful. Juvenile imagery—nursery rhyme characters, flowers, and animals—offers little help in dating as it was common throughout the entire time that Embroidered quilts were popular.*

American Quilt
Patterns

Tree of Life

The Tree of Life, also known as the Flowering Tree, is one of the earliest quilt patterns to appear in the American colonies. Its popularity had roots in the English enthusiasm for palampores, painted panels of flowering trees, that were imported to Europe from India. This trade began in the 17th century and continued through the mid-19th century.

When used as a quilt pattern, the Tree of Life was appliquéd, not printed, using the technique known as broderie perse. In this style of appliqué, the quilt maker cut images from painted or printed fabric, usually chintz (or in this case, palampores), and sewed them to the background fabric. To make a quilt, she would choose an image for the central tree, "root" it in a small mound or basket, and then add flora and fauna. Peacocks, pheasants, and monkeys were frequently included. Fascination with the Orient led to the inclusion of pagodas and Japanese tea houses. Many makers let their imaginations roam and combined on a single tree as many different leaves, fruits, and flowers as pleased them. The Tree of Life often appears at first to be a literal tree, but closer examination reveals the liberties taken in combining elements not found together in nature.

The quilt maker's Edenic collage was framed with one or more borders of chintz, either set square or on point. The borders appeared in varying widths, often made of chintz that had been printed specifically for this purpose. Sometimes the corners of the inner frame had pieced patterns, anticipating the repeat-block quilt style that replaced Center Medallions.

Unlike many patterns, the Tree of Life is almost always unidirectional. Its graceful, curvilinear forms and imaginative combinations of plants, animals, and human figures are best seen from the foot of the bed. Like its predecessor, the palampore, the Tree of Life is not necessarily quilted. Many examples are backed with a solid-color white cotton but lack batting and quilting. Others are bound without any backing. Regardless of whether or not they were quilted, they were intended as fine bedcovers. In all their forms, they are quite rare and considered extremely desirable to collectors.

Appliqué Tree of Life Quilt, Philadelphia, c.1800

The colors, design, and motifs on this quilt are typical for a Tree of Life.

Roses were appliquéd on a tree of a different species.

Clusters of appliqué chintz flowers and birds surround the central tree.

The background is discolored, but the quilt, a particularly early example, is too fragile to launder.

Size: 109 x 110in
2.75 x 2.80m
Value: $900–$1,200

Double-Framed Tree of Life Quilt, Massachusetts, *c.*1820

The red and blue border print repeats the tree pattern.

The two frames immediately surrounding the tree are made of fabrics printed specially for use as inner borders.

Several different types of blossoms grow from the central tree.

The small oval medallions are reminiscent of motifs seen in Persian carpets of the same period. It is unusual to find them in this type of quilt. The way in which they are arranged creates a very graceful border.

Size: 99 x 108in/
2.51 x 2.74m
Value: $8,000+

▶ *The proportions in this cotton Tree of Life example are more like a quilt and less like a palampore than many others. A more typical arrangement generally involves a larger center field with more clusters of appliqué creating borders, such as in the example opposite.*

◀ *In its day, this cotton quilt was a prime example of the Tree of Life. It has seen a hard life, though, and many of the appliquéd pieces are disintegrating. The poor condition is the only drawback to this quilt's valuation.*

Palampores

An authentic palampore from India is a single panel of painted or hand-printed fabric, usually a depiction of a flowering tree surrounded by birds, fruit, animals, buildings, or human figures. Alternatively, it showed a center medallion flanked by four corner motifs.

In India, palampores were used as wall hangings and bedcovers; when the English imported palampores, they used them as bed curtains as well as bedcovers. Imported palampores were very costly—which added to their allure and assured their position at the height of fashion. The original palette did not suit the English; the use of reds, browns, and blues on white was a modification for the English market.

It is important to understand the importance of the palampore as an antecedent to the American Tree of Life quilts and the center-medallion format. The casual collector is unlikely to find an 18th-century or early 19th-century palampore, however.

Nine Patch Quilts

The deceptively simple Nine Patch may be the most versatile of all quilt patterns. From the classic version of three rows of three equal-size square patches tumbles a kaleidoscope of patterns. It is astonishing how adaptable such a simple pattern can be.

Variations abound. The blocks may be set square or on point, with or without sashing. Individual patches may be subdivided into two or more triangles or into smaller squares (as in the Double Nine Patch, where alternate blocks are pieced as miniature Nine Patches). The relative size of the patches in the block may be different. Puss in the Corner is a traditional Nine Patch pattern with a large square as the center patch, small squares in each corner, and narrow rectangles between the small squares.

The choice of color and the distribution of light and dark shades yields dramatic results. The pattern may show an interesting alternation of positive and negative space.

Or the overall pattern may create a continuous chain effect. When set on point, carefully placed color variations can create secondary patterns.

Nine Patch quilts were made as early as 1800. This was one of the first pieced block patterns to emerge. Because of its simple and sturdy construction, Nine Patch was the pattern of choice for many utilitarian quilts and was often used by inexperienced quilters to practice their piecing. While the use of large-scale blocks helped the quilt reach completion more quickly and compensated for the quil maker's lack of expertise, it could also showcase exquisite fabrics and provide a field for superb quilting. Conversely, women made diminutive Nine Patches, especially those that included tiny triangles, to show their skill in piecing.

An adaptable and elegant pattern, the Nine Patch pattern illustrates especially well the idea that the whole is greater than the sum of its parts.

Nine Patch in Small Scale, origin unknown, *c.*1920

The small scale of the blocks gives room for many patches in which the patterned fabrics contrast well with the solid-color alternate blocks.

Some of the nine patches seem to disappear. They were made with fabrics that can barely be differentiated from the patterned ground fabric on which they are set.

In several instances, two, three, and even four blocks of the same color are placed next to each other.

Setting the small-scale blocks on point gives the quilt a nice diagonal movement.

The irregular edges suggest a lack of skill in construction.

Size: 66 x 72in/
1.7 x 1.8m
Value: $600–$900

"Puss in the Corner" Nine Patch, origin unknown, c. 1820

The addition of the narrow outermost border gives the quilt a subtle finish. This border was omitted from one edge to distinguish it as the end to go over the pillows.

The curvilinear shapes on the vines and ribbons printed in all the fabrics are an interesting counterpoint to the geometric shapes of the blocks. They add movement and grace to the quilt. Without them, it would be much more static.

The light-colored blocks create the illusion of a secondary pattern—a diagonal chain.

Size: 92 x 94in/
2.3 x 2.4m
Value: $2,000–$3,000

▲ *This variation of Nine Patch, in which the center block is larger than the others, is called Puss in the Corner. The use of just two cotton fabrics, with strong contrasting colors, is a bold interpretation of this somewhat airy pattern.*

◀ *The colors and scale of this cotton quilt are very pleasing. Better distribution of color would have made it a finer example, and greater variation would have contributed further to the twinkling effect created in some areas.*

Bindings

Binding refers to the method used to close the outermost edges of the quilt. There are two ways to bind quilts— self-binding or applied binding—and some variations in the technique.

Often, the quilt is self-bound. (In this usage, "self" means the fabric that is already in the quilt.) The United States and England have characteristic styles of self-binding. In the technique preferred in the United States, either the backing fabric is folded over the front or the front is carried to the back and the edge is hemmed. In England, the front fabric and backing are turned inward toward one another and the edges sewn together.

In the applied binding method, a separate strip of cloth is folded over the edges and sewn. The binding strip is often, but not necessarily, cut from the same material used in the quilt.

Regardless of technique, it is important to determine whether the binding is original or was replaced. The quilt's edges often receive the most wear, and replacing the binding becomes necessary to preserve the quilt. The technique and fabric in a replacement binding should be compatible with the age and aesthetic of the quilt.

It sometimes happens, however, that even an original binding appears less than an ideal match. In instances of mismatched bindings, the collector will want to look closely for signs of wear. This is necessary to determine whether the binding is original. A replaced binding, when done well with appropriate fabric, has minimal impact on the value of a quilt.

Wild Goose Chase Quilts

Perhaps inspired by the sight of migrating geese flying overhead, this simple representation of birds as small triangles has become a cherished standby for both strip and block designs.

Wild Goose Chase is a block pattern in which the bird triangles fly from each corner toward a square set in the block's center. Flying Geese is a strip pattern. In this version, the pieced blocks are set in a long column with the arrow points of the triangles all facing in one direction. It is a popular and often dramatic choice for sashing and borders *(see page 105 for an example)*.

In a more complex adaptation of Flying Geese, blocks of Wild Goose Chase produce lots of lively movement and intriguing secondary images. Usually, quilt makers chose a patterned fabric to create the geese in Wild Goose Chase, thus adding to the sense of wings in motion. Occasionally, they chose plain fabric to emphasize the secondary design.

Background fabrics, whether white or in colors, created an interesting contrast to the piecing.

Although examples from as early as the 18th century can sometimes be found, Wild Goose Chase achieved the zenith of its popularity in the mid-19th century. Collectors look for quilts that have many small triangles. The more geese the maker included, the more work she put into cutting and sewing, and—because piecing triangles is more difficult than piecing squares—the more skill she needed to complete the quilt top. Quilts for which care was taken to establish consistency of fabric and color and compatible choices of background present the harmonious compositions that bring high prices.

Astute collectors sometimes find examples of rare fabrics in these quilts. However, a scrap-bag Wild Goose Chase, with all sorts of colors and prints of different proportions, is an appealing, folksy bedcover.

Country Wild Goose Chase Quilt, origin unknown, *c.*1890

The overall red and blue color scheme gives this quilt a cheerful aspect.

The solid red of the sashing contrasted with the blue print works especially well.

The random use of light and dark triangles is indicative of a maker who worked well with the fabric scraps available to her.

Size: 78in/
1.98m square
Value: $400–$600

Lancaster County Wild Goose Chase Quilt, Pennsylvania, *c.*1890

Using just two solid colors adds greatly to the drama of this quilt.

Multiple secondary patterns are formed by setting the blocks without sashing.

Reversing the light on dark with dark on light in alternate blocks further adds to the patterning.

The white binding adds another frame and furthers the two-color contrast.

Size: 96in/
2.43m square
Value: $1,200–$1,600

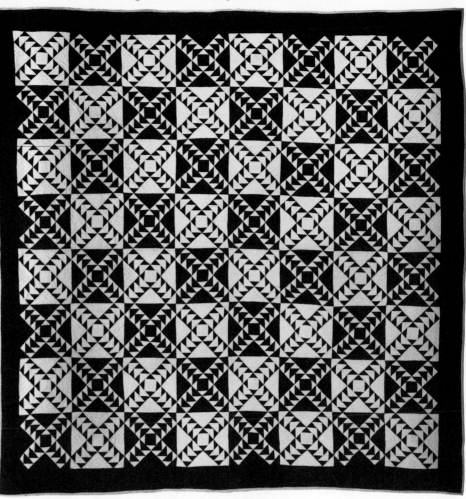

◀ *This cotton quilt is a good example of a country quilt without fancy quilting, piecing, or fabrics.*

▲ *This cotton quilt is an unusually large size for the late 19th century, when it was made. Often, modern buyers have difficulty finding collectible quilts that fit contemporary beds.*

▶ *The alternate color blocks, placed directly next to each other, create additional patterns throughout the quilt. The quilting is not fine, but the piecing and use of color compensate.*

Pine Tree Quilts

The Pine Tree pattern reflects the importance of forests—which were literally the backbone of this country. Pines and cedars were a critical resource for shelter, not only supplying the material from which houses were constructed but also providing fuel for the fires that warmed the home, heated water, and cooked the food. Trees also symbolize stability and rootedness. A new home's completion was marked by the planting of trees; a charming New England tradition called for the planting of "husband and wife trees" on either side of the entrance.

Additional evidence of the pine tree's significance is that it was selected as the image on the first coins minted in the colonies. In 1652, the Commonwealth of Massachusetts featured the pine on its shilling. It was also a symbol on early flags, including those for the first American warships. Given the importance of pine trees in our history, it is surprising that they did not inspire a wider range of quilt patterns; the designs tend to be generic representations of evergreens rather than depictions of specific pines.

This sharply abstracted image of a pine is very different from earlier, appliqué representations of trees such as the Tree of Life *(see page 98)*. Pine Tree is almost always done by piecing and is usually made of arrow-shaped trunks crowned with triangles for the leaves. Because the pattern has such stylized images, it is appealing even when sewn with large pieces and stitches. Most Pine Tree examples were made in the last 30 years of the 19th century. Whether finely or crudely made, the Pine Tree pattern is sought by collectors.

Traditional Pine Tree, origin unknown, *c.*1870

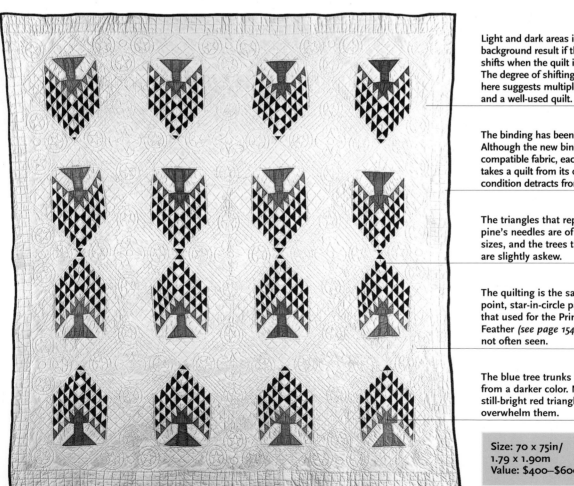

Light and dark areas in the white background result if the batting shifts when the quilt is washed. The degree of shifting visible here suggests multiple washings and a well-used quilt.

The binding has been replaced. Although the new binding is a compatible fabric, each step that takes a quilt from its original condition detracts from its value.

The triangles that represent the pine's needles are of uneven sizes, and the trees themselves are slightly askew.

The quilting is the same five-point, star-in-circle pattern as that used for the Princess Feather *(see page 154)*, which is not often seen.

The blue tree trunks have faded from a darker color. Now the still-bright red triangles overwhelm them.

Size: 70 x 75in/
1.79 x 1.90m
Value: $400–$600

Star Pattern Pine Tree Quilt, origin unknown, *c.* 1890

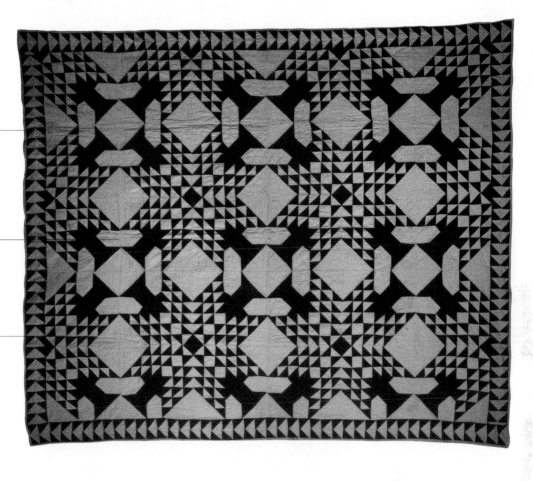

The pieced border, using the Wild Goose Chase pattern *(see page 102)*, continues the triangular theme of the quilt while adding some variation to the shapes.

The white patches around the tree trunks form hexagons and create a secondary pattern that suggests octagons, adding intricacy to the design.

The use of solid-color fabrics, which yield crisp distinctions between the positive and negative spaces, is especially effective.

Size: 74 x 84in/
1.88 x 2.13m
Value:$1,200–$1,600

◀ *The Pine Tree pattern, as in this example, is often set as rows of trees with their tops pointing toward each other. This is not ideal if the quilt will be displayed on a wall, but when used as a bedcover, the opposing images work well.*

▶ *The converging trees in this version of the Pine Trees create a dramatic combination of patterns.*

▲ *Traditionally, the Pine Tree pattern is made with solid colors on a white background. The counterpoint between the boldness of the color and the often finely detailed quilting is very striking. The graphic impact of this particular cotton quilt is exceptional. Turning the trees inward to form stars creates a complex and visually rewarding pattern. In this example, the technical quality of the stitching is far better than the piecing.*

Basket Quilts

Quilts that celebrated the simple geometry of the basket first appeared in the second quarter of the 19th century. They were made either by piecing, appliqué, or a combination of the two techniques. The Basket pattern probably developed among women attending agricultural fairs, where quilts were exhibited. Quilt makers offered pattern blocks for sale at these fairs, as well as trading them among themselves. Toward the middle of the 19th century, repeat-block patterns emerged as the dominant style among quilters. From that time forward, the Basket has remained a primary quilt pattern.

The basic form supports a surprisingly large number of variations. At its simplest, the body of the Basket is one large inverted triangle with its down-pointing tip flanked by two additional triangles to create a base. In another pattern, the Basket is made of squares set on point. The most complex examples create a large triangle from smaller triangles of contrasting colors to suggest latticework. In all cases, the handle of the basket is an appliqué arc, often sewn by machine, even when every other part of the quilt is sewn by hand.

Many examples of Basket quilts were made with large numbers of leftover fabrics in a wide variety of prints. An equal number were done with two or three colors on a ground fabric that clearly had been purchased specifically to be used in the quilt. Some examples have sashing that creates a secondary pattern.

Baskets have been made in many configurations, but they appear to have always been done in cotton. A Basket quilt made in any other fabric is extremely rare.

Colonial Basket Quilt, Pennsylvania, *c.*1880

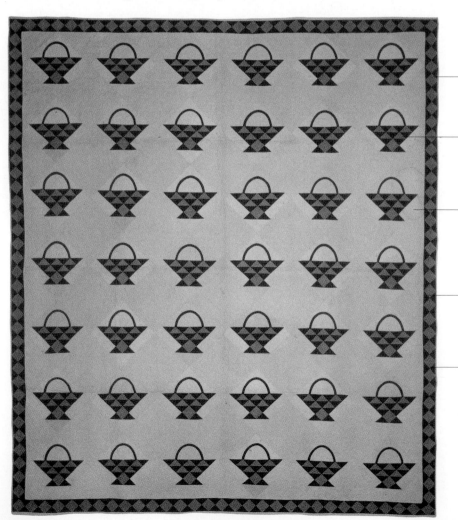

The use of the same two fabrics throughout indicates that they were probably purchased specifically for use in this quilt.

Each basket is set square but sits in a block that is set on point.

The entire background is made up of blocks on point—both the white spaces and the blocks on which the Baskets are pieced.

The pieced diamond border provides relief from the repetition of the average size baskets, which are all made from the same fabric.

The border introduces a related but different shape and provides a good frame for the pattern.

Size: 82 x 96in/
2.08 x 2.45m
Value: $700–$1,400

Zigzag Basket Quilt, origin unknown, *c.*1870

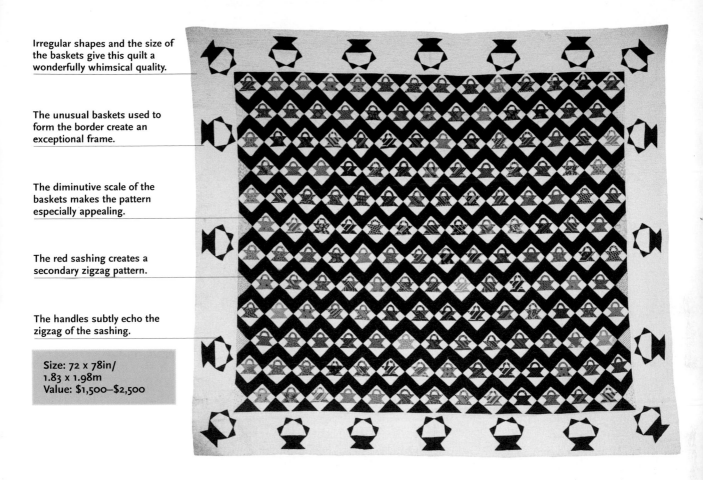

Irregular shapes and the size of the baskets give this quilt a wonderfully whimsical quality.

The unusual baskets used to form the border create an exceptional frame.

The diminutive scale of the baskets makes the pattern especially appealing.

The red sashing creates a secondary zigzag pattern.

The handles subtly echo the zigzag of the sashing.

Size: 72 x 78in/
1.83 x 1.98m
Value: $1,500–$2,500

◀ *This cotton quilt is well crafted. It was clearly intended as something finer than a scrap quilt. The piecing and quilting are both done with precision. Although well made and unified, however, the quilter's lack of imagination makes the quilt less of a find than the example above.*

▲ *This cotton Basket quilt is a very imaginative interpretation of a traditional pattern. While each basket is streamlined, the arrangement provides a great deal of visual interest.*

◀ *Both examples convey the image of a basket formed solely from triangles. The arrangement of the triangles, however, produces visual effects that vary considerably in terms of interest and originality.*

Log Cabin Quilts

The Log Cabin pattern became popular in the 1860s, during the presidency of Abraham Lincoln. It celebrates a key element of the Lincoln legend—his humble birth in an Illinois log cabin in 1809.

There seem to be an infinite number of variations on the Log Cabin quilt. In all examples, though, the basic block is a square surrounded by rectangular strips of fabric. The center square is usually red, which in quilt lore represents the fire in the cabin's hearth. The rectangular strips are meant to represent the logs from which the cabin was built.

For the most part, the visual interest of Log Cabins lies more in their color and overall pattern than in the quilting. In fact, the top and backing are often only tied or "tacked" together rather than actually quilted. In examples that are quilted, typically the stitching is done "in the ditch"—that is, the quilting is sewn in the seams between the logs and is barely visible.

In keeping with the building theme, the best-known Log Cabin variation is the Barnraising pattern. This pattern consists of concentric diamonds radiating from the center of the quilt, reminiscent of the frame on which a barn is built. Other popular variations have names such as Courthouse Steps, Split Rail Fence, Streak of Lightning, Straight Furrows, and Windmill Blades.

While the popularity of the Log Cabin pattern continues today, the greatest number of examples that are of interest to collectors were produced in the last 40 years of the 19th century. Quilts from that time may be made of cotton, wool, silk, or a combination of these fabrics. Log Cabin quilts run the gamut from rough, utilitarian bedcovers to extremely fine pieces meant for display.

Barnraising Log Cabin Quilt with Chevron Border, Pennsylvania, c.1870

The chevron border is a tremendous asset to this pattern. On a smaller scale, it repeats the basic pattern of the quilt and adds a great deal of drama.

The shades of persimmon and teal blue are unusual for the primary color scheme.

The red centers add even more warmth to the palette.

The quilt combines many wool challis fabrics very compatibly.

Size: 84in/2.13m sq
Value: $1,200–$1,800

Barnraising Log Cabin Quilt, New York, *c*.1900

Smaller-scale blocks would make this a more desirable example. A border would also enhance its value.

This is an unusual color scheme for a Log Cabin.

The two circles in the center of the quilt are a unique variation.

The quilt is in pristine, unwashed condition, which contributes to its value.

Size: 66 x 88in/
1.68 x 2.24m
Value: $600–$1,000

▶ *The relatively large scale of the blocks combined with the narrow shape of this woolen quilt give it a somewhat unfinished appearance. Had the horizontal sides ended with the corners of the diamond, it would have a more completed look. As it is, it appears as though the maker ran out of space for the design.*

◀ *The blocks of the border and the interior of this cotton quilt are in good proportion to one another. Overall, the color and scale of the quilt are well balanced.*

Pattern Names

Few patterns in the early 19th century had standardized names. More often, they were known by personal references, such as "Aunt Sara's basket pattern." Even at the end of the century, when periodicals circulated patterns, they were not always named. And even when pattern names were given and fairly well established, the names sometimes changed. Political and social events frequently stimulated such revisions. The Variable Star pattern, for example, was renamed Tippecanoe and Tyler Too, a reference to the 1840 presidential campaign slogan of William Henry Harrison.

When the business of publishing patterns proliferated in the early 20th century, names became more standardized, yet variations persisted. Whereas some designs, such as Irish Chain and Double Wedding Ring, are universally understood, many others continue to be known by more than one name. Mariner's Compass, for example, is also known as Chips and Whetstones and Rising Sun *(see page 118)*. These variations derive from individual preference and regional conventions. The stories or sentiments evoked by pattern names can be as interesting to collect as the quilts.

Log Cabin Quilts—Variations

Log Cabin blocks are constructed using a method different from most patterns. Instead of being built up seam by seam, they are sewn directly onto a foundation fabric, usually a square of cotton muslin. This gives the technique its name—foundation patchwork.

To create a Log Cabin with this technique, the first piece sewn down is the small central square that represents the hearth *(see page 108)*. Then the logs of the cabin are added in concentric rows that spiral around and out from the center. The quilter applies the fabric strip for each log upside down, sews it in place, folds it open so that the right side of the fabric shows, and then presses it. Another name for this process is pressed work. Crazy quilts *(see pages 60–63)* are also made on foundation blocks.

Many Log Cabin quilts made between the 1860s and 1880s were created from popular dress fabrics such as lightweight wools or wool blended with cotton or silk.

(Wool blended with silk is called wool challis.) These finely woven materials were supple enough to allow for delicate piecework. During the last decade of the 19th century, however, dress styles changed. They incorporated heavier wools, which were more difficult to manage when reworked into quilts. The Log Cabin examples made from these fabrics in the 1890s tend to be coarser, with wider strips.

Log Cabin quilt makers chose combinations of fabrics that included solid colors, floral or geometric prints, and plaids in both dark and light colors. The placement of light and dark colors, within each block and throughout the setting of the entire quilt top, yielded a remarkable array of dominant and secondary patterns. Some of these settings— Windmill Blades *(below)* and Straight Furrows *(opposite)*, for example—were made in such numbers that they have acquired their own standardized names.

Windmill Blades Quilt, Maryland, *c.*1870

The quilter pieced and designed this example flawlessly. It is in unused, pristine condition.

The hourglass pattern in the center of each block contributes depth.

The border incorporates the hourglasses from the half-blocks of the body of the quilt.

The quilt maker took great care in the placement of color throughout the quilt, but particularly in the border, where each fabric is repeated in the same sequence as in the blocks.

Size: 90in/2.29m square
Value: $2,000–$3,000

Straight Furrows Log Cabin Quilt, Pennsylvania, *c.*1870

The shades of purple and magenta have remained as vibrant as the day they were made. These colors were fairly common in wool challis fabrics of the late 19th century. They are highly susceptible to light damage, though, and few examples appear unfaded.

The sole flaw in this quilt is the workmanship of the border. It was evidently made a bit too large, resulting in puckering and unevenness.

The interior of the quilt is well pieced.

Size: 78in/1.98m square
Value: $800–$1,500

◀ *This pattern is equally well known as Pineapple Log Cabin. Both the pattern itself and the use of color give this cotton quilt exceptional, whirling movement. The Windmill Blades pattern is often made on a larger scale with fewer blocks. That, too, is very effective in creating the impression of whirling blades.*

▲ *More often, the variation of Log Cabin known as Straight Furrows is made with diagonal rows of light and dark color. When the light and dark zigzag, it is called Streak of Lightning.*

◀ *The quilt shown here, created in a pattern called Light and Dark, is one of a number of variations of the Log Cabin pattern.*

Delectable Mountains Quilts

Inspired by John Bunyan's classic allegory, *Pilgrim's Progress*, Delectable Mountains is among the most romantic of pattern names. In 1678, Bunyan wrote of the pilgrims: "They went then till they came to the Delectable Mountains…behold the gardens and orchards, the vineyards and fountains of water…" More than 100 years later, this expression of love for the land was recalled and the poetic phrase was bestowed as the name of this pattern.

Delectable Mountains is similar to Bear's Paw *(see page 134),* except that the small square in the pattern block was cut diagonally to form two identical triangles. As in Bear's Paw, smaller triangles, or sawteeth, extended from two sides of the large triangle. Delectable Mountains blocks were usually arranged in a center-medallion format, a setting of the pattern that created an especially dramatic effect. Right triangles with smaller protruding triangles were also sometimes used. In such cases, the result was an overall repeat-block pattern. When this arrangement was used, the pattern took the name Sawtooth.

Perhaps to honor the reverential tone of the name, Delectable Mountains were almost always finely made. Most examples come from the 19th century and exhibit a combination of fine stitching and beautiful fabrics. It is a favorite pattern among collectors.

Sawtooth Quilt, Maryland, *c.*1860

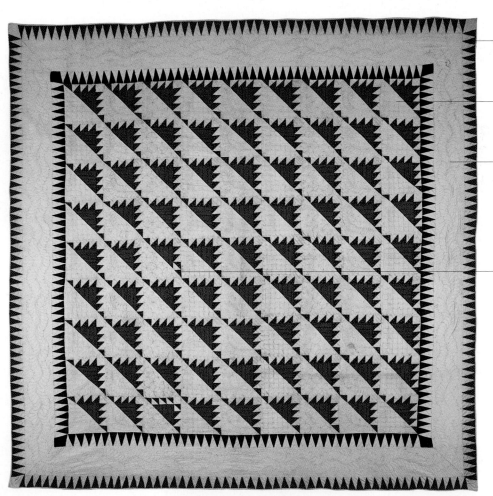

The piecing is particularly well done.

The maker alternated three different patterns within the white triangles, adding visual interest to the quilting.

The undulating feather quilting in the border provides a particularly graceful note.

Note the misplacement of two red triangles slightly to the left of the center of the quilt. Some would call this an intentional mistake but it is more likely an oversight *(see page 129).*

Size: 90in/2.29m square
Value: $1,200–$1,800

Delectable Mountains Quilt, origin unknown, *c.*1850

The corner of each concentric frame is quilted with the same half-wreath.

The fabrics on this example are mellow and varied.

Almost every white triangle has a different quilting pattern; the most unusual is the woman's face *(see detail photo below).*

The large clusters of printed flowers in the border fabric add another dimension to the frame.

Size: 92in/2.34m square
Value: $1,500–$3,000

◀ *This cotton quilt is very finely crafted, but in spite of the excellent workmanship, the pattern remains somewhat static. Greater variety of color or fabric would have made this a more interesting example.*

▶ *Many different quilting patterns are used within the white blocks of this quilt. The most unusual, by far, is the profile of a woman's face, perhaps the quilter's self-portrait.*

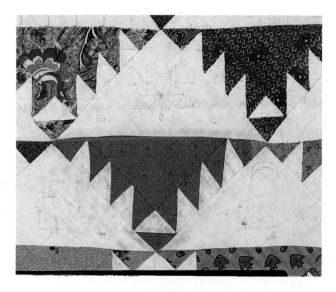

▲ *When the blocks are set as they are in the cotton quilt above, the resulting pattern is usually more dramatic than the arrangement in the Sawtooth example opposite. As seen here, multiple radiating and crisscrossing secondary patterns are formed by the more innovative setting.*

Irish Chain Quilts

Unlike other quilt patterns that have multiple names, Irish Chain seems to be the sole standard for this design. But what was it about a group of squares set to form a chain that evoked the Irish? It is intriguing to wonder how such a consensus could have formed around a name that bears no resemblance to the visual experience of the quilt. Curiously, this was one of the few patterns of the "English" (anyone not Amish) that were made by the Amish in Lancaster County.

Perhaps because of the dynamism of its simple geometry and relative ease of assembly, Irish Chain was one of the earliest patterns employed. It remained popular throughout the 19th and 20th centuries and promises to endure long into the 21st. The pattern sometimes consisted of single chains, in which single squares were set to form diagonal lines across the surface of the quilt.

More often, double or triple chains were made. Typically, these chains were composed of rows of two or three squares set to form crossing diagonals throughout the quilt; occasionally, the chains ran straight up and down.

There is considerable range in the value of Irish Chain quilts. As this is a fairly common pattern, even a novice buyer can easily compare examples and become familiar with the range of possibilities. Value is determined by assessing the size of the squares that make up the chains, the choice of color and fabrics, the quality of the piecing and quilting, and the presence of any special border treatments. In general, smaller squares require more skill to assemble and are therefore more valuable. An ordinary example in excellent condition may be found for as little as a few hundred dollars; a prime example can cost several thousand.

Double Irish Chain Quilt, Maryland, c.1860

The pristine, unwashed state of this quilt is a plus.

Adding stars to the setting blocks adds greatly to the visual interest of this quilt.

The printed border adds more color to what is otherwise a simple red and green quilt, and the ribbon twining through the flowers complements the strong diagonal rhythm of the chains.

The waffle quilting pattern is sturdy but standard and prevents this from being an exceptional example.

Size: 100 x 112in/
2.54 x 2.84m
Value: $900–$1,400

Double Irish Chain Quilt, origin unknown, c.1890

The maker combined an interesting mix of indigo prints that contrast well with the solid red they abut.

Although the red and blue blocks are quilted in parallel diagonal lines, the in-between blocks are filled with a herringbone pattern that is not often seen.

Some would feel that using a solid-color fabric in the blocks between the chains, rather than the small, figured print, would have provided bolder contrast.

The lack of a border gives the quilt an unfinished quality.

Size: 77in/
1.96m square
Value: $300–$600

▶ *The maker of this cotton Double Irish Chain used prints throughout, rather than printed chains and a solid ground. Unfortunately, the combination detracts from the crispness of the design.*

◀ *The large overall size of this cotton Double Irish Chain quilt keeps the size of the chain blocks from being out of scale. Had they been smaller, though, it would be an even more valuable piece.*

Cotton Seeds

Many people believe that if one holds a quilt up to the light and can see dark spots in the batting, that person is actually seeing cotton seeds. They believe that the seeds are proof that the quilt was made early in the 19th century. This belief is mistaken on several counts.

First, the dark spots are probably not cotton seeds but rather fragments of other parts of the plant. They are proof not of age, but of inexpensive, poorly cleaned cotton. Various grades of cotton batting were sold throughout the 19th century. The less expensive the batting, the more impurities remained in it. And despite the advent of the cotton gin in 1794, many people—particularly those in rural areas—still had to clean cotton by hand. This also led to inconsistencies in quality.

Additionally, the specks are found even in quilts that were made well into the 20th century. In other words, contrary to popular belief, dark spots in the batting give little or no indication of a quilt's age.

New York Beauty Quilts

As with many quilt names, a location name does not necessarily reflect a pattern's place of origin. The New York Beauty acquired its name around 1932, when Mountain Mist, a batting company, printed on its batting wrappers the pattern and directions for a simplified version of an older 19th-century design. The company may have chosen the name to suggest a tie to New York and its tradition of sophisticated quilt designs, but no evidence exists that it was one of the state's favorites.

Examples of the older design, with names such as Rocky Mountain Road, Sunset, and Crown of Thorns, were made throughout the 19th century, some as early as 1800. Many of these quilts were made in rural Tennessee and Kentucky by women who used the household duty of making blankets as an opportunity for artistic expression. The Mountain Mist version of this spiky design proved very popular and remained one of their staple offerings for more than 30 years.

Even in a simplified form, New York Beauty is an exquisitely difficult design to cut and piece, and it must have been even more challenging to draft before printed patterns existed. The entire design is pieced, not appliquéd, and the construction has to be perfect for the blocks to line up and form the master design. Some quilt makers raised the stakes even higher by setting the entire design on point, which results in stunning diagonal graphics. As befitting a tour de force of piecing, the background areas are usually filled with elaborate quilting patterns. When made with bold solid colors on a white background, the graphic appeal is among the highest.

The pattern is composed of circles, arcs, and slim triangles with needle-fine points, all of which test the skill of even the most experienced seamstresses. A quarter-circle rests in one corner and is banded by an arc set with numerous long slender triangles. The points of each triangle must be cut and sewn with great precision for the design to work. When set without sashing, the banded quarter-circles form an image of a radiating sun. A true New York Beauty, however, is set with sashing that employs the same slender triangles as in the block. The corners where the sashing intersects are typically pieced with smaller versions of the sun or with a pattern that echoes that shape.

The intensity of skill required to accurately construct these quilts makes the best examples highly desirable to collectors. New York Beauty quilts that have been designed with harmonious colors and executed with precise piecing and fine quilting command good prices. Even cruder versions, in which the points are blunted or the piecing is a bit off, can be effective and collectible.

New York Beauty Quilt, origin unknown, c.1880

Concentric quilted arcs repeat the circular forms of the orange blocks.

The triangles in the central sunbursts and around the orange blocks are particularly fine. Each one is quite small and ends in a needle-fine tip.

The brown spaces between the circles seem to recede while the orange circles advance, creating a sense of depth.

The quilt's color combination is unusual and very striking.

Size: 78 x 98in/
1.98 x 2.49m
Value: $3,500–$4,500

Pale Palette New York Beauty Quilt, origin unknown, *c.*1920s

The solid-color stars in the centers are a nice counterpoint to the printed fabrics used throughout the rest of the quilt.

The choice of fabrics is unusual, particularly the red, black, and yellow prints around the circles. They are surprisingly Art Deco for this 19th-century design.

The overall pattern works very well. When examined closely, though, it is evident that most of the triangles end in blunted tips. Crisp, needlelike points would make this a more desirable example.

Size: 73 x 77in/
1.85 x 1.95m
Value: $600—$900

▶ *The pale palette in this cotton quilt is very unusual; this pattern is almost always made in bold colors. It is purely a matter of individual preference as to whether the unusual colors are an asset or a drawback.*

◀ *This cotton quilt is well constructed and has tremendous visual movement. The quilting patterns contribute to the effect as much as the piecing does.*

Quilt Sizes

People are often surprised to find that the earliest quilts, those dating from the late 1700s through 1830, are consistently the largest. Beds and quilts were home- and handmade on an as-needed basis, and sizes were not standardized as they are today. Beds were often built to accommodate several members of the family and were consequently large.

The practice of families sleeping together probably developed for practical reasons—warmth in cold seasons and limitations of living space. Beds were also built to be high off the ground in order to keep slumberers well above the drafty floor. In fact, step-stools were often required to climb into them. Because early quilts draped all the way to the ground in this period, most of them measure more than 10ft/3m square.

By the mid-19th century, sleeping styles changed. The three-quarter bed, smaller than a modern double size, became prevalent, and quilt sizes shrank accordingly. The relatively small size of late 19th-century quilts should not put the collector off, however. Accommodations for contemporary beds are easily made with pillow shams and dust skirts—and a small size can be an asset when displaying a quilt on a wall.

Lone Star Quilts

The names Star of Bethlehem and Lone Star are used interchangeably for this pattern. Equally fine examples were made with a single star, as well as a central star surrounded by smaller ones. In either instance, the pattern's name does, in fact, refer to a celebration of Texas, the Lone Star State. The first appearance of this pattern in the 1830s slightly predates the fall of the Alamo in 1836, the founding of the Republic of Texas, and the use of the Lone Star as a symbol of the new republic on its flag.

In its most basic form, this pattern features a central star without surrounding stars, appliqué, or other designs, and in terms of quilt chronology may be considered an adaptation of the Central Medallion format. Many examples do contain smaller stars and/or other motifs surrounding the central one, but these are considered variations on the classic design. Another variation, the Broken Star, connects the points of the main star with a repetition of each arm of the star to form a zigzag ring around the central motif. This variation makes a particularly dramatic presentation.

Traditionally, the Lone Star is made of diamond-shaped pieces that radiate from the center in concentric rows. It is critical that the eight patches that form the star's center be exactly equal in size, precisely cut to 45-degree angles, and perfectly aligned. If they aren't, the error will be compounded row by row, and the remainder of the quilt will be increasingly out of kilter.

Beginning in the 1920s, Lone Star kits became available for purchase. More often, though, these quilts started with homemade patterns and carefully chosen fabrics and represented the pinnacle of the quilt maker's art. Skillful manipulation of color, prints, and fabric can create the illusion of pulsation—a true starburst.

Flower-Bordered Lone Star Quilt, origin unknown, *c.*1860

The curved shapes of the appliqué border provide an attractive counterpoint to the severe geometry of the stars.

This unique design combines traditional stars with a "homegrown" interpretation of flowerpots.

Note how the two different shapes of the flower stems create a graceful line that forms a subtle swag.

The arrangement of colors successfully creates a pulsating effect in the central star.

Size: 96in/
2.44m square
Value: $3,000–$4,000

Shirting Print Lone Star Quilt, Pennsylvania, *c.*1890

The condition of this quilt is very desirable: it is pristine and unwashed.

The red circle at the center of the main star sets off the orange and yellow that surround it. It may have been placed there as decoration or to conceal a flaw; in either case, it is a clever solution.

The shading from red to pink to white is nicely modulated and creates the effect of a starburst.

The quilt lacks a border, which would have provided a helpful frame.

Size: 80in/
2.03m square
Value: $900–$1,400

◀ *The central star in this cotton quilt is surrounded by smaller stars and half-stars, all of which are pieced; the pots of flowers in the border are appliquéd. Solid-color and calico fabrics are combined throughout the quilt.*

▶ *Close examination of the center star here indicates that it is evenly pieced, a critical element in the construction of the entire quilt.*

▲ *Each star in this cotton quilt is made of diamond-shaped blocks and combines solid and calico-print fabrics. The background fabric is a shirting print. Each surrounding star is pieced and then appliquéd to the ground. The unusual red circle in the center of the main star is the only piece in the entire quilt that is not diamond shaped.*

Drunkard's Path Quilts

Drunkard's Path emerged in the third quarter of the 19th century. Oddly enough, the pattern was associated with the Women's Christian Temperance Union. In fact, it used the pattern for many of its fundraising quilts. It is also surprising that the pattern's name did not suffer the same fate as that of another—Wandering Foot—which was renamed because of bad connotations: people feared it would provoke wanderlust. Superstition demanded that a Wandering Foot quilt never be included among quilts for a bride. Children, especially boys, were not allowed to sleep under these quilts. It is a wonder that no such superstition was attached to Drunkard's Path; somehow this meandering pattern didn't inspire the belief that proximity to it could induce unwholesome thirst, and the name has endured for well over a century.

The pattern's bold and simple shapes do not invite fine quilting, and the design's success relies on its overall graphic impact. The scale of the indiviudal pieces is especially important. When well done, a tension exists between positive and negative space that adds visual interest. This pattern is most effective when made with two sharply contrasting colors, and many vibrant examples were executed in red or indigo and white. Sashing is rarely used between the blocks. Instead, the blocks abut to create a tumbling diagonal pattern with a staccato visual rhythm that makes it easy to imagine how the name came about.

Many middle-range examples of Drunkard's Path quilts can be found; a truly fine example is rare. While the pattern can be visually interesting, it is not usually sought by the most sophisticated collectors.

Traditional Drunkard's Path Quilt, Pennsylvania, *c.*1890

This is a charming, if somewhat prosaic, example of a country quilt, with nothing to give it exceptional value to a collector.

The fabrics work well together. The use of a red-on-black print calico for the paths is a nice echo of the black-on-red print of the border.

Although the color contrast is good on this quilt, using prints softens the edges between the patches and weakens the crispness of the design.

Size: 75in/
1.9m square
Value: $500–$700

Red on White Drunkard's Path Quilt, Pennsylvania, *c.*1890s

Using only two colors without prints produces strong contrast in this quilt.

An unusual herringbone border adds tremendously to the desirability of this quilt.

The relatively small scale of the blocks forms more paths than is typical for this pattern.

The quilting is rudimentary, and there are errors in the piecing: some of the red patches, for example, are turned the wrong way.

Despite its flaws, this example makes an extremely effective, bold statement.

Size: 82in /
2.08m square
Value: $900–$1,300

▲ *While this cotton quilt is not finely constructed, the equal proportions of red and white, along with the large number of paths, enhance the dynamism of its pattern.*

◀ *This is a straightforward cotton version of a traditional pattern without any original touches. This would not be a collector's find.*

Humility Patch

An interesting notion in quilt lore holds that a quilt maker purposely placed something askew in her work to demonstrate her humility. By this choice, quilters acknowledged that only God was perfect and purposely demonstrated their own imperfection.

Although this idea has been repeated countless times, no factual documentation exists to support it. Nineteenth-century diaries and interviews with more contemporary quilters have not produced a single verification of this legend. When asked in an interview about her intentional mistake, one contemporary artisan responded with, "What mistake?"

It is more likely that mistakes were simply that—errors that occurred because quilts are made by limited humans. Typically, quilts are worked on in sections, so it is easy to overlook misplacement of a single piece in the overall design. This type of detail is often more obvious when viewing the quilt from a distance, which is not the way most 19th-century quilters worked. They probably did not see any irregularities until a finished quilt was put on a bed. To correct an error at that point would mean not only opening the seams of the individual patch but also unpicking and restitching the quilting.

Pinwheel Quilts

A square cut on both diagonals to form four inward-facing triangles is an ancient pattern that is known all over the world. It is found in many cultures, in architectural elements, in mosaic decorations, on pottery, and on clothing and other textiles. The image has tremendous visual tension and is remarkably versatile.

Quilt makers in the United States and in England adopted the design early on. Several quilts that have survived from the 18th century used the figure in their central sections and borders. Originally called Mill Wheel or Water Wheel, by the 19th century the pattern name had evolved from the industrial to the playful and was known almost universally as Pinwheel.

Because the pattern is so simple, it works in any setting—square, on point, or diagonal, with or without sashing. It also works in any scale; changing the size of the blocks simply changes the impact of the pattern. When made from large blocks, it shows off the graphic movement of the triangles; when the blocks are small, it showcases the quilter's piecing and sewing skills. Pinwheel is equally effective when made in two boldly contrasting colors or when made with every patch in a different fabric.

Many variations of Pinwheel developed over the years. A version with four broad flat blades was popular in New York and New England. A geometric version of triangular blades attached to a central square developed in the late 19th century. In the 20th century, a version appeared with curved blades around a central circle, resembling a child's toy pinwheel. The design remained popular into the 1940s.

As with many patterns of basic design, the choice of fabrics, size of blocks, placement of elements, and sewing technique usually make the telling difference in value. Early examples of Pinwheel quilts in excellent condition rarely come on the collector's market. When they do, they command high prices. Many later—but less desirable—Pinwheels are available with costs determined by size, color, and workmanship.

Stuffed-Worked Border Pinwheel Quilt, origin unknown, c.1830

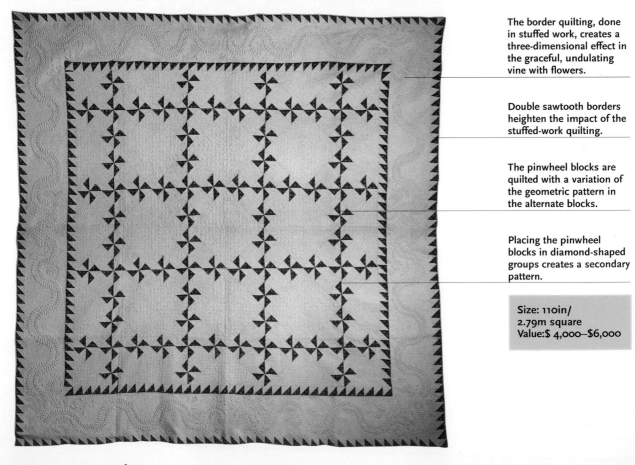

The border quilting, done in stuffed work, creates a three-dimensional effect in the graceful, undulating vine with flowers.

Double sawtooth borders heighten the impact of the stuffed-work quilting.

The pinwheel blocks are quilted with a variation of the geometric pattern in the alternate blocks.

Placing the pinwheel blocks in diamond-shaped groups creates a secondary pattern.

Size: 110in/
2.79m square
Value:$ 4,000–$6,000

Utilitarian Pinwheel Quilt, Pennsylvania, *c.*1900

Setting the blocks with sashing and in rows on point creates a secondary zigzag pattern.

This quilt is made of heavy wool, probably from overcoats and men's suits, and was most likely made for warmth.

This type of quilt would usually be tied or tacked. Here, the maker put in the extra effort to quilt it.

In spite of the utilitarian intent, the maker used care in placing light and dark colors to create an overall pattern that would add interest.

Size: 68 x 77in/
1.73 x 1.95m
Value: $500–$800

▶ *This woolen quilt falls at the opposite end of the spectrum from the example opposite. It is interesting to see so clearly that the same pattern can be made for either utilitarian purposes or as a very fine quilt.*

◀ *The maker of this cotton quilt spared no effort in either piecing or quilting. All the needlework in this quilt is well done, but the quilting is especially fine. Note, however, the placement of the triangles in the corners of the sawtooth borders. In spite of the maker's technical expertise, she did not achieve a uniform ending in each row of triangles. This is particularly evident in the upper left inner border, where she had to add a tiny strip to fill in the space. This difficulty does not affect the value of the quilt, especially when the remaining work is of such high caliber.*

Quilting Bees

Nostalgic tales about quilts often mention that they were made by groups of women at festive quilting bees. While the main purpose of these gatherings was to speed the production of quilts, there's much more to the story.

Beyond the need to complete quilts, these gatherings—known in the 19th century as quilting frolics—were an important aspect of social life. On the frontier, where people lived far apart in harsh circumstances, a quilting bee allowed women to exchange gossip and political news, as well as share patterns and recipes. Toward evening, the men arrived for a meal, which was followed by games and dancing. Much matchmaking took place. Legend has it that when the last row of quilting was about to be done, the married women stepped back and the young misses took over. The woman who put in the last stitch was believed to be the next to marry.

Toward the middle of the 19th century, the purpose for which the quilts were made—and therefore the purpose of the get-togethers—changed. Earlier, quilts were made to provide warmth for family and friends. Later, they were made as charitable contributions for the needy, and the former frolics became high-minded, task-oriented, church-affiliated events for women only.

Bear's Paw Quilts

The basic blocks of the Bear's Paw and its cousins, Goose Tracks and Turkey Tracks, appeared early in the history of quilt making, about 1800. All three designs use a combination of appliqué and piecing to achieve a five-part basic shape. Most blocks have a center square, with a figure at each of its points made of several diamonds, triangles, and/or smaller squares. From this basic construction, variations appear. The Bear's Paw usually has four smaller squares with pointed triangles "clawing" off the main square. The Goose Tracks variation has four figures of wider triangles or diamonds. Turkey Tracks has a shaved center square and elongated triangles at the tips.

These designs accumulated various names over the years. Bear's Paw was said to be popular first in the Ohio/Pennsylvania border region, perhaps originating there. Turkey Tracks was originally called Wandering Foot and was reputed to have caused those who slept beneath a quilt bearing its pattern to leave home and family behind. These quilt designs acquired names evoking animals, farms, and rural life in general, in the late 19th century, probably when the first published patterns appeared.

Some of the earliest Bear's Paw and Turkey Tracks quilts were constructed of imported, red and green, roller-printed fabrics and have a very sophisticated look. In the late 19th century, the Bear's Paw and its variants were made in indigo blue and white and other two-color combinations. These quilts exhibit very striking compositions and have vaulted ahead of other examples in the estimation of many collectors. In the early 20th century, Ohio and Indiana Amish made especially good use of this pattern with bold, solid colors. These quilts command high prices now.

This set of designs lends itself to endless manipulations of color, playing off dominant and recessive colors. When made well, with typical calicoes—or even from scraps— these quilts with animal names can have great charm and appeal. Bear's Paw and variations made from feedsacks during the 1930s and later are still plentiful and can be found at modest prices.

Simple Bear's Paw Quilt, origin unknown, c.1860

The green print fabric has changed color significantly from its original shade. This detracts from the quilt's value.

There is slight soiling, which is most readily visible in the white fabric. This is a drawback that can be remedied fairly easily.

For some, the presence of a border on only three sides is a minus.

The white blocks are quilted with pinwheels, which seem too elaborate in the context of the simplicity of this quilt.

Size: 70 x 80in/
1.78 x 2.03m
Value: $400–$600

Multipatterned Bear's Paw Quilt, Winchester, Virginia, *c.*1870

This may be one of the most complex versions a Bear's Paw in existence. Whether the sophisticated patterning was intentional will never be known.

The wide, deep indigo binding provides a nice contrast to this otherwise two-color quilt.

This example is well quilted and finely pieced.

Size: 81 x 91in/
2.06 x 2.31m
Value: $1,000–$1,800

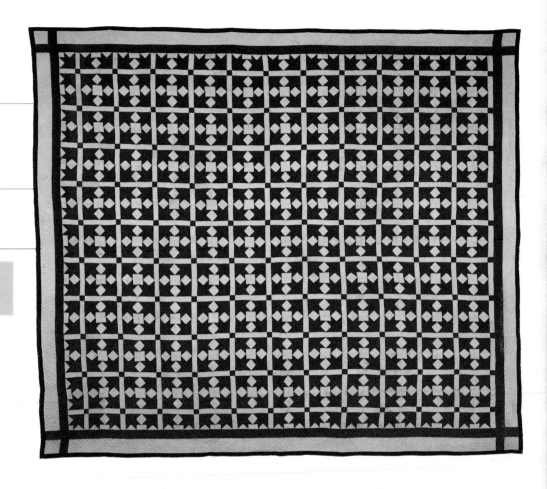

◀ *This cotton Bear's Paw quilt is bordered on only three sides. The borderless edge would be placed at the pillow end of the bed. Today's collectors, who often hang quilts on walls, may find such a treatment less appealing than a four-sided border. When hanging, the quilt does not have as complete a frame.*

▶ *The detail illustrates clearly the three ways of seeing patterns in this complex quilt: as a Bear's Paw pattern; as a white square surrounded by diamonds; and as a series of outward-pointing arrows.*

▲ *This entire quilt is made from a brick-color calico and plain white cotton, with a wide blue calico binding. The close spacing of the blocks gives this quilt the appearance of three distinct patterns. For the predominant Bear's Paw, the calico pattern appears to have been placed on the white ground. Another way of viewing this is to see a white square surrounded by four white diamonds on the calico ground. Alternatively, a third pattern can be seen as a series of four calico arrows pointing to the corners on a diagonal from the center.*

Whig Rose Quilts

Whig Rose, more than any other pattern, has been known by a great variety of names. The 1828 presidential campaign, when the Whig Party was established to oppose Andrew Jackson's Democrats, is credited with inspiring the pattern. But apparently both political sides claimed it, for Whig Rose is also known as Democratic Rose. It has been called Colonial Rose, Harrison Rose (in reference to William Henry Harrison, the president elected in 1840), and Mexican Rose (in commemoration of the Mexican War of 1846–48). Regional fondness for this pattern is evident in the names Ohio Rose, Kentucky Rose, and Texas Rose. A popular variation hearkening back to the pattern's horticultural origins is called Rose of Sharon.

While the various patterns have much in common, they also diverge somewhat. The aspects they share are a central floral form from which radiate at least four undulating vines with leaves and repeats of the central flower. The stylized flower does not evoke a multipetaled cultivated rose but rather the flat, open blooms of a wild rose. Elaborate appliqué borders frequently embellished the central rose design with variations of the primary

flower growing from baskets, flowerpots, or stems. Swag motifs, with or without appliquéd tassels, were popular, as well. The palette seen in most examples was red and green, with bits of other colors for highlight and counterpoint.

Most examples of this pattern were made in the 1840s and 1850s, the time when the Whigs were struggling for power. The party did not continue after 1855, which was probably the time when the pattern known as Whig's Defeat came into being.

Whig Rose is typically executed in the four-block style that was popular with most appliqué patterns of the mid-19th century. This style allowed the quilt maker considerable background material on which to display elaborate quilting patterns surrounding the appliqué images. Most often, these graceful and dramatic appliqués were made as best quilts to be used only on special occasions. Because they were not made for everyday use, they did not have to sustain multiple washings and usually do not show much wear. Contemporary collectors have reaped the benefit: many fine examples have survived from among the number that were made.

Rose of Sharon Quilt, Pennsylvania, c.1860

The large amount of white background allows the fine quilting to show to its best advantage.

The small scale of the Roses of Sharon does not give this quilt the exuberance that this pattern usually has.

The quilting stitches are tight throughout, with a wreath around each floral motif.

The details in pink and yellow work effectively to soften the red and green.

The appliqués around the primary flowers appear disjointed—particularly the green arcs.

Size: 72 x 88in/
1.83 x 2.23m
Value: $1,200–$1,600

Whig Rose Quilt by Abigail Hill, Indiana, *c.*1857

The trapunto wreaths are beautifully stitched. Their shape echoes the curved forms of the primary design, as well as the sinuous border vines.

The folded triangles along the edge, known in the 20th century as Prairie Points, provide a nice anchor of color.

The border is masterfully designed. The vines grow out of the pots on each horizontal side of the quilt and blend well with the main pattern.

The quilt has several species of birds, an element not often seen.

Leaving an opening in the border for the appliqué date was a clever innovation.

> Size: 70 x 80in/
> 1.78 x 2.03m
> Value: $7,000–$10,000

▶ *The design, quilting, and appliqué come together wonderfully in this outstanding cotton quilt.*

◀ *The construction of this quilt is interesting. Rather than sewing all of the appliqué onto one solid ground, the quilter sewed it onto triangular and diamond-shaped blocks that were then assembled.*

Distinguishing Trapunto from Stuffed Appliqué

There are two basic techniques for creating three-dimensional design in quilts: trapunto and stuffed appliqué. Although the terms are often used interchangeably, the techniques are distinctly different. Trapunto requires the more exacting skill, but both require fine needlework ability. They are seen in only a small percentage of quilts, usually from the early to mid-19th century.

Trapunto refers to stuffed quilting. In this technique, the outline of desired shapes is sewn, and then extra batting is inserted through the backing of the quilt to produce higher relief in selected areas of the design. The quilt maker painstakingly inserts the batting by pushing it with a needle through a tiny slit in the backing or between the threads of a loosely woven backing. The stuffed area takes on a rounded form without an extra layer of fabric.

Stuffed appliqué refers, of course, to appliqué rather than to quilting Extra batting is laid under the appliqués before they are sewn to the ground fabric.

Floral Wreath Quilts

Appliqué bedcovers have a centuries-long tradition in Europe. The distinctly American contribution to the form is the red and green appliqué patterns that were popular between 1840 and 1880. During this time, broderie perse appliqué *(see pages 42 and 98)* using chintz was replaced by what quilt historians refer to as "conventional appliqué"—patterns composed of solid and printed cottons.

These developments paralleled advances in technology and industry. By the early 19th century, numerous fabric mills had opened in the United States. Widespread domestic manufacturing of cloth offered two boons to quilters: it brought the price of fabric within reach of middle-income women, and it freed up the time women had previously devoted to spinning, weaving, and dying their own homespun cloth. With technological advances, more women had the wherewithal in time and materials to make quilts for decoration as much as for warmth. Artistry for art's sake was no longer solely the domain of the very wealthy.

Botanical motifs dominate appliqué quilts made in the mid- to late 19th century, and the Floral Wreath pattern is an important form in this category. As with the Whig Rose pattern *(see page 144)*, no attempt was made to render flowers realistically. Rather, they were stylized and merely suggested a particular form.

Most Floral Wreath quilts from this era feature predominantly red and green motifs on white backgrounds. Pink, orange, and yellow appear as accents for floral centers or buds. Although patterns were not yet being published during the heyday of this style, they were circulated among groups of women or copied from examples exhibited at agricultural fairs—which accounts for the definite stylistic similarities of many examples. It is also not unusual to find that the boldness of the color and simplicity of the shapes of the appliqué contrast with delicate stitching patterns. Floral Wreath quilts remained popular well into the 20th century. Later versions are easily distinguished from earlier examples by their pastel colors and more realistic flowers.

President's Wreath Quilt, Pennsylvania, *c.*1860

The appliqué flowers on the border alternate between two patterns. Nearly every one of the tulip shapes has a different design done in reverse appliqué.

Each side of the border has a finely appliquéd and embroidered bird shaped like a sewing bird, a pincushionlike ornament that was popular in Southeast Pennsylvania.

The quilter used different quilting patterns within each of the floral wreaths.

The orange centers of the flowers on the wreaths are reverse appliqué.

Size: 80 x 100in/
2.03 x 2.54m
Value: $1,000–$1,400

Floral Wreath Quilt by Marie Landis, Lancaster, Pennsylvania, *c.*1870

The border treatment is original and highly labor intensive.

Each of the repeated flowers is reverse appliqué.

Each wreath contains a different design. The large red and blue birds probably represented husband and wife.

The quilter used embroidery and layers of appliqué to provide detail throughout the quilt. In addition to many imaginative flowers, there are also birds, roosters, and a butterfly.

Size: 65 x 94in/
1.65 x 2.39m
Value: $7,000–$10,000

▶ *The pattern and colors in this cotton quilt are extremely rich and vibrant. Each of the motifs within the wreaths appears to be an original design. The quilt maker, Marie Landis, intended the pattern to be viewed from the sides of the bed, but the overall pattern is so intense that it bears looking at vertically as well.*

◀ *This quilt is unusually large for the period in which it was made, making it suitable for many contemporary beds. At first glance, this quilt appears to be the most standard version of a circular wreath. Closer examination, though, reveals subtle, innovative details.*

Reverse Appliqué

The word "appliqué" is derived from the Latin word *applicare*, which means to fold or to fasten down. Two forms of appliqué may appear: traditional appliqué and reverse appliqué.

In traditional appliqué, a fabric shape is laid on top of the background material and sewn in place. This technique was first known as "laid-on work." Many classic appliqué quilt patterns—Sunbonnet Sue *(see page 160)* and Baltimore Album *(see page 54)*—rely on this technique.

Reverse appliqué is inlaid work. In this technique, two or more layers of fabric are sewn together. Then, working from the top down, patterns are cut from each successive layer. The cut edges of each layer are turned under and sewn to the one beneath with tiny, nearly invisible stitches. The sculptural quality of reverse appliqué creates a fine impression of depth.

Reverse appliqué is rarely seen in American quilts, but when it appears, it is the mark of a fine needleworker.

Flower Basket Quilts

Flower baskets were one of the earliest themes in quilt patterns. Baskets or pots of flowers were fashionable in other decorative arts as well. Theorems—paintings of baskets or compotes of fruit or flowers stenciled on paper or velvet—were a popular art form for many women in the 1830s and 40s. The theme appeared as well on stenciled or hand-painted furniture. Not surprisingly, it cropped up in quilts, and the popularity of this charming and versatile image has continued unabated through 200 years of American quilting. Flower Basket quilts, more than many patterns, can vary from the ornate and elaborate to the most basic.

The earliest examples appeared as appliquéd center medallion designs and used the broderie perse technique. (Broderie perse is a form of appliqué in which an image is cut from a print fabric, usually chintz, and then sewn to the ground.) Soon after, quilt makers began to form lattice baskets from appliquéd strips of patterned or solid-color fabrics such as chintz or calico, broadcloth or poplin. Later examples combined appliqué with piecework and served as either a central motif or as repeat blocks. There is no limit to the combinations available to imaginative quilt makers in expressing their enthusiasm for a colorful container and flowers.

It is difficult to categorize Flower Baskets since the construction techniques, fabrics, forms, and time period in which they were made vary so widely. An engaging contrast in styles exists between flowers that are pieced, and thus usually composed of geometric shapes, and those that are appliquéd and employ curvilinear forms. Although both attempt to achieve the same image, they result in extraordinarily different effects. Similarly the dyes and fabrics commercially available during the era in which such quilts were popular exerts a tremendous influence on the colors used. The earliest examples, from the late 18th century through the 1830s, appear in chintzes of rose, blue, and brown hues. From the 1840s through the 1880s, this pattern was often carried out in cheerful reds and greens. By the 20th century, all combinations were possible, but most quilters chose to include subtle pastels.

Cotton Quilt, c.1866 (origin unknown)

Mrs. Barker's affection for her son is evident in this buoyant quilt, which she signed in cross-stitch, "Presented to A.S. Barker by his mother H.M. Barker 1866." The rosy color scheme may suggest that she hoped for a girl, but assigning specific colors to the sexes was not in fashion until the 20th century.

The tiny baskets at the sashing intersections add delightful detail.

Using solid colors in the border and for the flowers in the baskets enriches the quilt's visual impact and balances the calico fabrics used elsewhere.

Although the technique in the quilt is not extraordinary, the exuberant design more than makes up for it.

Size: 71 x 79in/
1.80 x 2m
Value: $3,500–4,500

Quilt from Pennsylvania, signed "Sarah Geddes 1860"

Note how the frames around each basket form a diagonal grid across the quilt.

Placing the baskets with flowers in a diamond pattern in the center creates an unusual twist. Also notice that those baskets lack handles but have ears.

The quilt lacks a specific border, but the quilter continued the frames around the baskets as half forms, which provided a good compromise.

The quilt lacks the exuberance that makes many floral basket quilts so appealing, a fact that diminishes its value.

Size: 84 x 94in/
2.13 x 2.39m
Value: $800–1,400

▶ *The signature and date that appear on this quilt enhance its value. The fabrics confirm the date; that is, they were available in the 1860s, so we can assume that the quilt was made at that time.*

◀ *This pattern is particularly rich and full. The appliquéd basket handles, flowers, and border are wonderfully balanced against the geometric forms of the baskets.*

Turkey Red

The term "Turkey red" often comes up when quilts are discussed and refers both to a color and to the dye process used to create the color. The process, which was begun in 1829, involved two steps. The cloth to be dyed was first soaked in oil, then boiled with madder root to produce a rich, vibrant tone. (The roots of the madder plant have been used to create a red dye at least since the Middle Ages. The red tones in the famous Unicorn tapestries were achieved with madder.)

The resulting red color was popular throughout the remainder of the 19th century, in part because it was not subject to bleeding. Repeated washings often turned it to a mellow shade of rose, but it did not run.

Robbing Peter to Pay Paul

This graceful pattern contains an optical surprise. When rendered in two contrasting colors and set side by side, the blocks create the impression of overlapping circles. This "square peg in a round hole" effect results from the skillful manipulation of the blocks' symmetry. A segment from one block is "robbed" from the adjoining block—and vice versa. The pattern's effect depends, as well, on confident choices of color. Many quilt patterns—Tumbling Blocks (*see page 138*) is another outstanding example—rely on secondary patterns arising across the seams of the basic blocks, but few are as simple, bold, and effective as Robbing Peter to Pay Paul. The greater the number of blocks in the quilt, the more the sense of movement will be from the curved pieces intertwining with one another.

This pattern was known as early as the second quarter of the 19th century. Traditionally, it is made of only two colors, although a third fabric is sometimes introduced for the border. The classic nautical combination of indigo and white is striking and recalls the woven coverlets that were popular around the same time.

Like the stripped-down patterns of the Lancaster County Amish quilts (*see pages 76–79*), Robbing Peter to Pay Paul is one of many 19th-century designs that calls to mind the question of whether or not the early makers realized the overall effect of combining these blocks. Did they intend the strong figure-to-ground illusions created by abutting the blocks? Were they aware of the multiple patterns that would be created? Or were these happy accidents for them, and now, for us?

Robbing Peter to Pay Paul Quilt, origin unknown, *c.*1830

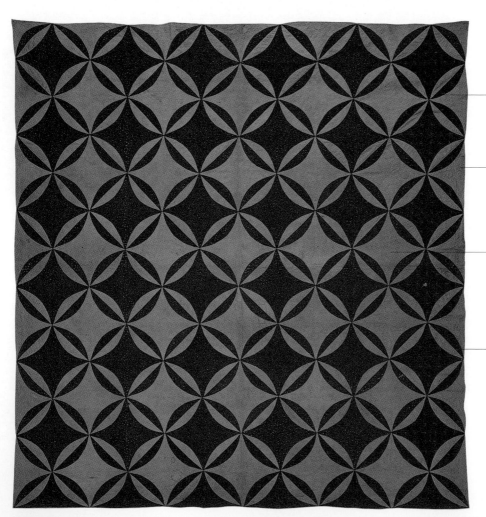

The condition of this quilt leaves much to be desired. It is soiled, and damage to the red fabric can be seen. The red may be too fragile to risk washing the quilt.

A border would have been effective in containing the pattern, especially given the large scale of the blocks.

Each open space has a different design, all done with stipple quilting. Unfortunately, the very fine quilting is obscured by the dinginess.

Both the colors and scale contribute to the sense of motion in the design—the light colors seem to come forward, while the darks recede.

Size: 88 x 96in/
2.24 x 2.45m
Value: $200–$400

Robbing Peter to Pay Paul Quilt, Pennsylvania, *c.*1840

This example is in pristine, unwashed condition.

The white flowers in the print add lightness and also echo the white of the alternate blocks.

The border print is an unusual fabric showing a stormy seacoast, but its colors skillfully echo the ones in the quilt top.

The quilting is a clamshell pattern. It is surprising to find this and the seacoast imagery of the border on a quilt made inland.

Size: 90in/2.29m square
Value: $1,000–$1,800

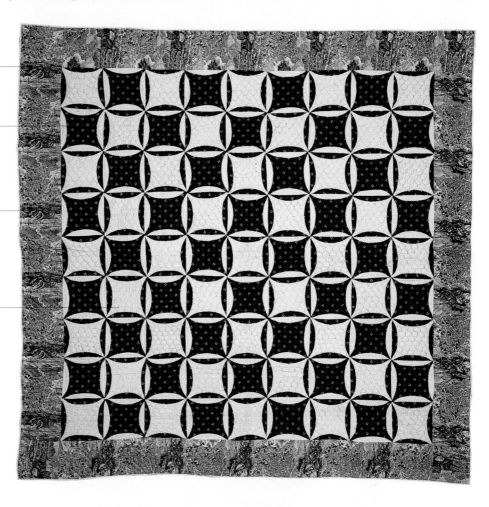

◀ This cotton quilt, only 10 years older than the one shown above, demonstrates the telling difference for the collector between a quilt that has been well conserved for more than a century and a half, and one that has not. While some neglect and wear can be overcome when dealing with antique quilts, there are real limits in such a case as this. An attempt to bring back some of its original virtues would probably destroy it.

▲ The quilt maker showed great sensitivity in her choices of color and fabric. The overall effect is one of harmony and cohesiveness.

◀ The scene printed on this fabric is most unusual. The tones subtly but effectively carry through the colors of the body of the quilt.

Robbing Petter to Pay Paul   151

Alphabet Quilts

A great rarity, but a delightful one, the Alphabet quilt was inspired by the needlework samplers that young girls in the 18th and early 19th centuries made to practice their sewing skills. Typically, alphabet quilts simply enlarge the sampler lettering used to mark household linen; some also replicate the composition of samplers and imitate the foursquare look of cross-stitch.

From a quilt maker's point of view, the letters of the alphabet add up to an awkward number of figures—26 symbols cannot be treated as 26 individual blocks and then neatly arranged into five rows of five blocks or into six or seven rows of four. Women devised a number of ingenious schemes to answer this challenge. One solution was to squeeze two letters into one block. Another was to cheerfully boot a few out to the border.

The earliest Alphabet quilts appeared in New York State in the 1830s; these examples usually feature letter forms pieced from red or indigo fabrics. Other varieties of lettering also appeared on New York quilts and were used to spell out a variety of messages, such as the names and ages of makers and recipients, dates, locations, Bible verses, pithy sayings—even memorials for the departed. (By the 1850s, these elements had migrated from the centers to the borders of New York quilts.) In the 1840s, appliqué was gaining popularity as a needlework technique, and quilt makers in Pennsylvania and other northeastern states swiftly adopted it for Alphabet and other letter quilts. While lettering continued to appear into the late 19th century—it was often used when inscribing the maker's name, for example—the sampler-inspired quilt style faded from production.

Alphabet quilts experienced a revival in the 1920s, this time in a different form. Patterns appeared for embroidered letters, often with appliqué or embroidered animals and other figures, in the newly popular pastel colors. These blocks were included in quilts for children, giving the young recipients an amusing way to learn their ABCs.

Because so few Alphabet and early lettered quilts were made, prices tend to be quite high. The commercial embroidered children's quilts that were marketed later are appealing and were made in large enough numbers to be more available—and more affordable.

Signed Alphabet Quilt, Pennsylvania, dated 1917

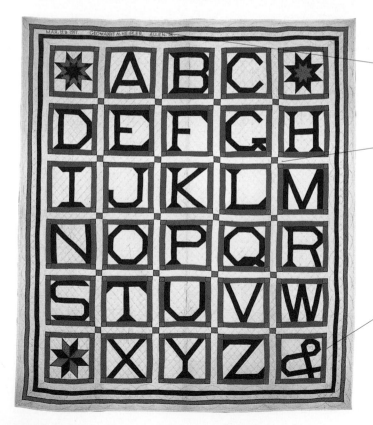

The inscription of two names indicates that this quilt may have been made as a wedding gift.

The Nine Patch blocks between the letters add visual interest.

Three of the corners on this quilt bear star patterns. Without corner blocks, many makers had difficulty placing the last letter. In this case, the quilter used the corner blocks, but chose not to carry the star into the fourth corner.

Size: 77 x 90in/
1.95 x 2.29m
Value: $10,000+

Appliqué Alphabet Quilt, origin unknown, dated 1930

While this is a very nice example of its type and charming for a child, it is most likely made from commercial patterns.

The appliqué images are more prominent than the embroidered letters; this adds more color and variety overall.

The images accompanying each letter indicate that it was made for a child. Earlier examples without such word pictures—like the example opposite—were probably made for adults.

**Size: 54 x 78in/
1.37 x 1.98m
Value: $800–$1,200**

◀ igned "Mar 12th 1917. Geo & Addie M. Heipler. Allen, Pa.," this is a prime example of a fine cotton Alphabet quilt. It is well made and in pristine, unwashed condition.

▲ This cotton quilt is signed "Grandmother Maler 1930." Youth-size quilts such as this are not made as often as Crib or full-size. This size proves practical either for a child's bedcover or as a wall hanging.

◀ The appliqué images that accompany the letters make this a much stronger visual statement than if the work had all been done with embroidery.

Double Wedding Ring Quilts

The quilt pattern most closely associated with the 1930s is the ever-popular Double Wedding Ring, which consists of interlocking circles. Each circle is made of squares of fabric—when this pattern developed, these would usually have been small-scale prints from dresses, aprons, or feedsacks. The printed fabrics are most often offset by complementary solid colors in the four squares forming the intersection of the circles.

Double Wedding Rings were sometimes made entirely of solid-color fabrics, but these were the exception. It is interesting to note that the Wedding Ring is one of the few patterns from the "outside world" used by the Amish in the Midwest. The Amish, of course, used a consistent palette of solid colors on a dark background. The

difference in this pattern when executed in the Amish palette is quite striking.

Double Wedding Ring quilts are almost always finished with scalloped edges. Rarely does the border extend beyond the outermost circles. Although scalloped edges make it more difficult for a collector to hang a quilt, this was not the purpose for which the piece was made: scalloped edges fall gracefully over the sides of a bed.

While many collectors seek more unusual patterns, there is a steady market for familiar patterns like the Double Wedding Ring. This pattern continued to be made into the 1950s, but the garish colors of the later examples make them less desirable for collectors.

Prairie-Point Edged Quilt, origin unknown, *c.*1930

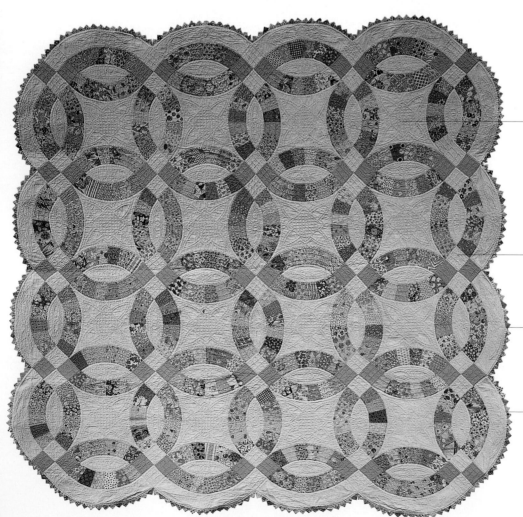

This example has finer quilting than is usually seen on a Double Wedding Ring.

A secondary, repeating design known as Four Patch appears in solid green and white pieces that form squares at the intersections of the rings. The solid colors only for these patches are especially attractive.

Prairie points, particularly of this diminutive size, add to the quality and value of this quilt.

There is an overall harmony and pleasing consistency to the many fabrics incorporated in this example.

Size: 72 x 74in/
1.83 x 1.88m
Value: $600–$800

Straight-Border Edge Quilt, origin unknown, *c.*1930

Many of the prints used in this example feature patterns with too large a scale for the size of the pieces for which they were selected.

The pattern might have appeared more cohesive had there been greater consistency to the spacing of solid and printed fabrics.

This example is nicely quilted, with four-lobed, stylized flowers that fill the open white spaces.

This quilt is more easily hung for display than most Wedding Rings because it has a straight-edged border.

Size: 77in/
1.96m square
Value: $300–$600

▶ *This cotton quilt was made from fabrics typical of the late 1930s. A better selection of fabrics with an eye for combining colors and patterns would have improved the finished product.*

◀ *The edging on this cotton quilt is finished with folded triangles known as Prairie Points, and solid–color and printed fabrics are used consistently throughout.*

Signed and Dated Quilts

The vast majority of collectible quilts were neither signed nor dated. In cases in which they were, a reference might or might not be to the maker and the time she completed her piece. The name could be that of the person for whom the quilt was created. The date could refer to an important event, such as a birth or marriage.

In some instances, the pattern was chosen to commemorate an earlier event. For instance, a Double Wedding Ring quilt dated 1900 would not have been created in 1900 because the pattern did not exist until some 30 years later. Familiarity with fabrics and quilting styles can thus provide some valuable hints as to whether a date indicates when a quilt was made. Names are more difficult to determine. A male name is generally assumed to indicate the recipient, not the maker, although men were known to make quilts. Inscriptions appear in ink; embroidery; within the quilting; or, least often, in appliqué.

In rare cases, when a maker was especially proud of her work, she left no doubt as to who she was and how long she worked on her opus. For making such a choice, the collector is grateful to her, because it provides invaluable information about time frames for many other quilts.

Dresden Plate

The Dresden Plate quilt pattern takes its name from the German city that was renowned for manufacturing highly decorated porcelain. These quilts combine piecing and appliqué to create circular motifs and use a multiplicity of designs for the wedges that make up the circles, imitating Dresden plates. The plate edges can be finished as simple circles, but more often they feature scallops or points.

One of the three patterns most often seen in quilts of the 1920s and 1930s, the basic Dresden Plate shape was used as early as 1785 and continued to appear in late 19th-century Crazy quilts. The earlier versions were shaped like wheels with spokes of wool, or later, of silks and velvets. The design also owes a debt to the Fan pattern that became popular during the late 19th century. The modern version of the Dresden Plate was published in the 1920s with some simplification of the older design. Women were encouraged to make the newly named pattern from floral prints, using up scraps of other sewing projects. The plate elements could be placed on the background cloth without embellishment, or they could have added sashing and fancy borders, or more floral spokes resembling ice cream cones.

Dresden Plate quilt components were available in preassembled kits, but most examples were made from purchased patterns in dress prints, and increasingly, in the 1930s, from printed feedsacks. Some quilt makers used a combination of solid pastel-colored fabrics for their Dresden Plates, an approach that makes an effective variation and appeals greatly to contemporary tastes. The pattern remained popular throughout the 1940s, when quilters tended to incorporate fabrics of brighter and bolder colors.

As examples of quilts in this pattern exist in the thousands, many people continue to buy the pleasant but more ordinary examples for bedroom use, where the color schemes fit decorating trends. To be collectible, a Dresden Plate quilt needs to be distinguished by some combination of special characteristics, including interesting fabrics, unusual placement of elements, small and numerous plates, and excellent construction and quilting.

Prairie Point Border Dresden Plate Quilt, origin unknown, c.1940

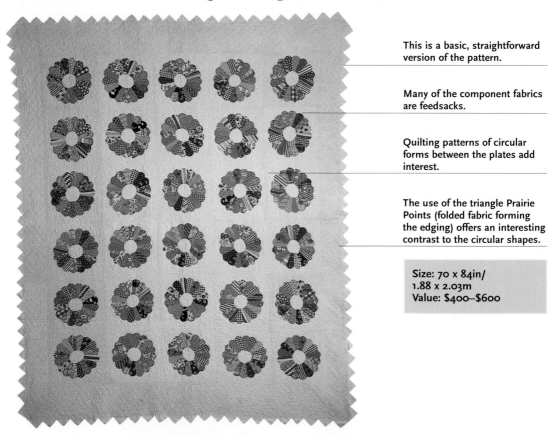

This is a basic, straightforward version of the pattern.

Many of the component fabrics are feedsacks.

Quilting patterns of circular forms between the plates add interest.

The use of the triangle Prairie Points (folded fabric forming the edging) offers an interesting contrast to the circular shapes.

Size: 70 x 84in/
1.88 x 2.03m
Value: $400–$600

Dresden Plate Quilt, Pennsylvania, *c.*1930

The use of color and the fabric selection create a pleasing and harmonious overall effect.

The swirling grid provides a secondary pattern, offering a Pinwheel pattern between the plates and an undulating ribbon effect in the border. This breaks up the repetition of the circles.

The solid-color fabric of the grid and inner circles contrasts attractively with the printed fabrics of the plates.

While the quilting is not superb, it adds to the movement of the pattern by echoing the blue semicircle shapes.

Size: 74 x 80in/
1.88 x 2.03m
Value: $700–$1,000

▶ *The sophisticated cotton pastel-colored quilt at right combines the Dresden Plate with subsidiary Pinwheel and ribbon-effect patterns.*

◀ *It is interesting to contrast the white, open centers of the plates in this cotton quilt with the blue centers in the example opposite. While neither treatment is inherently more desirable than the other, the use of open centers in this quilt creates depth by making the plates stand out against the ground fabric.*

Feedsacks

Beginning in the 1890s and continuing through the 1950s, thrifty housewives transformed the sacks that held feed, flour, sugar, salt, and fertilizer into clothing, quilts, and household linens. In economically depressed eras and areas, the sacks were an essential source of fabric. Eventually, the practice became so commonplace that sacking companies made bags from printed cottons suitable for recycling into household items and included instructions for removing their ink or paper labels.

Careful examination of quilts of this period in patterns such as Sunbonnet Sue, Overall Sam, Double Wedding Ring, and Dresden Plate reveal many feedsack prints. In fact, prints abounded. The patterns might be floral, figural, geometric, striped, plaid, or paisley. Some women bleached or dyed the sacks, while others purchased sacks that had been commercially dyed a solid color.

For the most part, solid-color feedsacks were used for the backs of quilts and prints for the tops. Feedsacks varied in size from several inches to several feet. The cottons were durable, colorfast, and usually a coarse weave. The sacks were sewn with heavy thread and thick needles that left punctures in the fabric—and these holes are strong evidence that a fabric comes from a recycled sack.

Grandmothers' Flower Garden

Grandmother's Flower Garden was one of the most popular patterns of the 1920s and 1930s. While it is often given short shrift by quilt collectors today, this pattern is extremely labor-intensive to execute. The entire quilt is made of separate hexagons. Colored groups of hexagons are joined together in a larger hexagon to form the "garden." There is no solid background between the gardens—every inch of the quilt is composed of adjoining hexagons.

For quilts of this pattern, each piece was typically made by folding and securing the fabric over a template of stiff paper or cardboard, which was not removed until the top, batting, and back were assembled. This method was also used for Honeycomb or Mosaic quilts of the early 19th century. Despite the painstaking labor involved in this technique, the quilts do not necessarily command high prices. The fact that Grandmother's Flower Garden quilts are readily available outweighs other factors in determining their value.

Most Grandmother's Flower Garden quilts were made of cotton in pastel shades. While the gardens themselves are a combination of solid-color and printed fabrics, the "garden paths" between them are usually a solid color, most often white. Diamond-shaped "gating" outlining the gardens can provide a striking contrast, giving the gardens the appearance of added dimension.

Most examples of this pattern are fairly standard in format, and collectors seek those occasional examples that are out of the ordinary. A traditional Flower Garden can easily be found for several hundred dollars. Only the finest examples, those made with tiny pieces or forming an unusual overall pattern, are likely to sell for more than a thousand dollars.

Traditional Grandmother's Flower Garden Quilt, origin unknown, c.1930

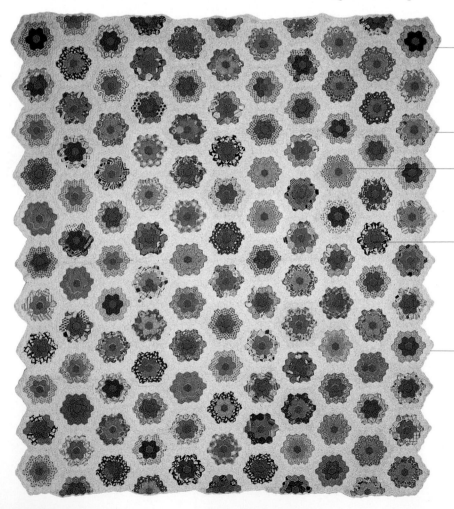

The unused condition of this quilt makes it desirable.

The format is the most traditional for the Grandmother's Flower Garden pattern, limiting its value to collectors.

The colors blend well together.

The scale of the gardens is a little smaller than is typical of this pattern, which is a plus in terms of value.

Most examples of this pattern have scalloped edges along all four sides. This example has scalloped edges only along the long sides, a shortcut necessitated, perhaps, by the size of the quilter's bed.

Size: 72 x 84in/
1.83 x 2.54m
Value: $400–$900

Gated Grandmother's Flower Garden Quilt, origin unknown, *c.*1930

This is an extraordinarily complex variation of this pattern, making the quilt much more valuable than most Grandmother's Flower Garden examples.

The gardens can be seen as a background for the Tumbling Blocks pattern, while the diamonds are also arranged in a repeating star-shaped pattern.

The red diamond "gating" provides a dramatic outline to each of the subpatterns.

The unused condition of this quilt adds to its desirability.

This example is larger than most quilts of the period, making it more readily usable on a contemporary bed.

Size: 80 x 100in/
2.03 x 2.54m
Value: $900–$1,500

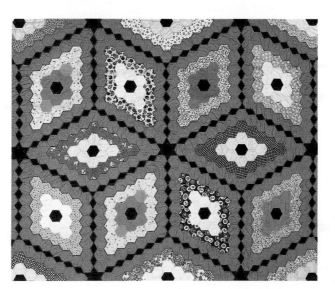

◀ *The hexagons in this cotton quilt are made of both solid and printed fabrics. The edges are scalloped on only two sides, and the quilt is in pristine, unwashed condition.*

▲ *In this cotton quilt, both solid and printed fabrics are used throughout, and the gardens are unusual in their diamond-shaped design.*

◀ *A Tumbling Blocks pattern is incorporated in the design, as well as a star pattern formed by the combination of six of the diamonds surrounding each garden. A small red star makes a hub for each of these larger stars.*

Sunbonnet Sue – Overall Sam Quilts

The original Sunbonnet Sue made her debut in the 1880s, when she appeared in published patterns as a simple outline of embroidery. Illustrator Bertha Corbett, in a 1902 primer, modified the image to Sue's now-familiar large dress and bonnet. In 1912, the first versions of this pattern were offered in *Ladies Home Journal*. The pattern reached its zenith of popularity in the 1920s and 1930s, but the endearing appliqué figure has endured.

Part of Sue's appeal, and that of her rarer friend, Overall Sam, is her shyness. Despite the thousands of quilts made in this pattern, Sue's face—always in profile and always shielded by the brim of her ever-present bonnet—has never been seen. Sam, sometimes called Bill, is always depicted with his back to the viewer.

In even the simplest versions, the fabric of Sue's clothing varies in each block. Mothers were urged to use remnants of their daughter's dresses to fabricate Sue's clothing, creating a keepsake. Many examples used feedsack prints. Embroidery added detail to Sue's wardrobe.

As the design was offered nationally in kits or commercial patterns for decades, there are no regional variations. Sunbonnet Sues appeared by the thousands as full-size quilts. Crib-size variations are slightly less common. A few quilts depict both Sue and Sam. Collectors seek only exceptional variations with great detail, many activities, unusual placement of elements, small scale, and fine workmanship. A traditional example, though, makes a pleasing child's bedcover for a modest price.

Overall Sam Appliqué, Pennsylvania, *c.*1930

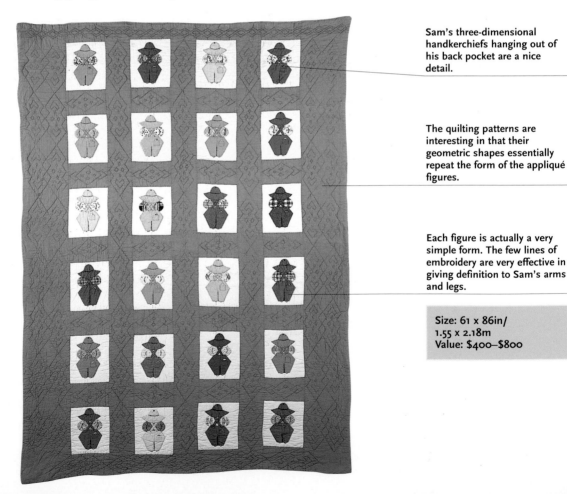

Sam's three-dimensional handkerchiefs hanging out of his back pocket are a nice detail.

The quilting patterns are interesting in that their geometric shapes essentially repeat the form of the appliqué figures.

Each figure is actually a very simple form. The few lines of embroidery are very effective in giving definition to Sam's arms and legs.

Size: 61 x 86in/
1.55 x 2.18m
Value: $400–$800

Sunbonnet Sue Appliqué, Pennsylvania, *c.*1930

Only Sue is appliquéd; all the other elements are embroidered.

Sue is wearing many feedsack prints, typical of the day.

It is rare to find an example such as this, in which Sue is engaged in a different activity in each block, with varied animals and flowers.

The embroidery is more detailed than usual, giving Sue fingers on her hands and shoes on her feet. (Usually, Sue is an ambiguous female figure, with or without arms, but almost never with hands or feet.)

Size: 68 x 94in/
1.73 x 2.39m
Value: $800–$1,200

◄ *This cotton quilt is the most standard format of Overall Sam. He is almost always an ambiguous figure seen from the rear.*

▲ *The lively interpretation of Sunbonnet Sue on this cotton quilt is unusual. It took a great deal of imagination, as well as skill, to design and embroider so many different motifs, all of which appear to have been done freehand.*

◄ *Appliqué and embroidery are combined in each block to give detail to the figure of Sue and the activity in which she is engaged.*

Yo-Yo Quilts

Yo-Yo bedcovers are categorized as quilts, although technically, they are not. Rather than being layers of fabric and batting quilted together, each individual yo-yo is made from a circle of fabric—either a print or a solid. The outer edge is turned under and basted, then the thread is pulled tight to form a smaller, puckered circle and tied off. Typically, each finished yo-yo is about the size of a half dollar. To make a bedcover, the yo-yos are tacked together with easy, overhand stitches, making an airy, open grid of crinkled buttons with the cheery exuberance of confetti.

Its construction, and the lack of a backing, make Yo-Yo quilts difficult to hang on a wall. The best way to display one is on a bed over a solid-color sheet or blanket. The solid fabric will twinkles through the spaces between the circles, creating an almost stained-glass effect. Yo-yos

enjoyed a heyday in the 1930s and 1940s, and they were used in other household decorations, too. Table runners and pillow tops were popular at the same time as the bedcovers.

Today's collectors show little appreciation for this pattern. Nevertheless, a great number of Yo-Yo quilts were produced, and people do continue to make, buy, and enjoy them. Only the most extraordinary examples sell for more than $600–$800. Versions with small yo-yos, and examples in which the colors are placed to form patterns, are much more desirable to collectors. In the case of secondary patterns, the design usually takes the form of yo-yos made from prints sewn within square- or diamond-shaped grids made of solid-color yo-yos. Another variation involves pulling the basting thread tight enough to make the fabric circle a small wrinkled ball rather than a bumpy, but relatively flat, button. This is known as a Popcorn Spread.

Square-Grid Yo-Yo Quilt, unknown origin, *c.*1930

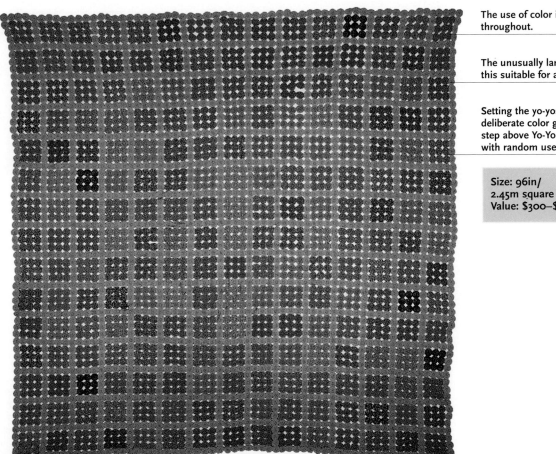

The use of color is harmonious throughout.

The unusually large size makes this suitable for a modern bed.

Setting the yo-yos in a deliberate color grid puts this a step above Yo-Yo quilts made with random use of color.

Size: 96in/
2.45m square
Value: $300–$600

Multipattern Yo-Yo Quilt, origin unknown, *c.*1935

The bold use of color is unusual for this pattern, which is usually done in pastel shades.

The solid-color outlines around the printed yo-yos add further visual interest and cohesiveness.

The extraordinary attention to additional patterns, both Tumbling Blocks and Stars, puts this Yo-Yo in a class by itself.

Size: 80 x 92in/
2.03 x 2.35m
Value: $800–$1,500

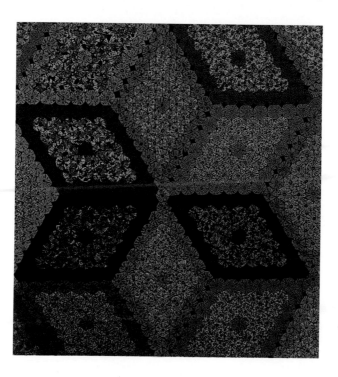

◀ *Although this cotton quilt is a bit drab, the blend of neutral colors allows for use in many decorating schemes.*

▲ *This cotton example is one of the most imaginative, well-executed expressions of this pattern.*

◀ *Not only is the arrangement of yo-yos in a diamond shape unusual, but they have been combined to form stars and tumbling blocks, as well.*

Where to See and Buy American Quilts

Where to See

Almost anywhere in the United States, you will be able to locate examples or collections of antique American quilts. The following institutions have quilt collections. It is best to contact the institution in advance of a visit to find out how and when you can see the quilts. Many state and local historical societies also have quilt collections.

The Birmingham Museum of Art
2000 8th Avenue North
Birmingham, Ala. 35203
205-254-2566

Anchorage Museum of History and Art
121 West Seventh Avenue
Anchorage, Alaska 99501
904-343-4326

Arkansas State University Museum
Arkansas State University
State University, Ark. 72467
501-972-2074

The University Museum
University of Arkansas,
Fayetteville, Ark. 72701
501-575-3466

American Museum of Quilts and Textiles
110 Paseo de San Antonio
San Jose, Calif. 95112-3639
408-971-0323

Los Angeles County Museum of Art
American Quilt Research Center
5905 Wilshire Boulevard
Los Angeles, Calif. 90036
213-857-6083

The Oakland Museum
1000 Oak Street
Oakland, Calif. 94607

The Denver Museum of Art
100 West 14th Avenue Parkway
Denver, Colo. 80204
303-575-2196

The Henry Francis du Pont Winterthur Museum
Route 52, Kennett Pike
Wilmington, Del. 19735
302-656-8591

Daughters of the American Revolutiom
1776 D Street NW
Washington, D.C. 20006
202-879-3241

National Museum of American History
Division of Textiles
Smithsonian Institution
Constitution Avenue between 12th and 14th Streets, NW
Washington, D.C. 20560
202-357-1889

The High Museum of Art
1280 Peachtree Street NE
Atlanta, Ga. 30309
404-733-4400

Bernice H. Bishop Museum
1525 Bernice Street
Honolulu, Hawaii
808- 847-3511

Mission Houses Museum
553 South King Street
Honolulu, Hawaii 96813
808-531-0481

The Art Institute of Chicago
Department of Textiles
Michigan Avenue at Adams Street
Chicago, Ill. 60693
312-443-3696

Indianapolis Museum of Art
1200 West 38th Street
Indianapolis, Ind. 46208
317-923-1331

Indiana State Museum and Historic Sites
202 North Alabama
Indianapolis, Ind. 46202
317-232-1637

Spencer Museum of Art
The University of Kansas
Lawrence, Kans. 66045
913-864-4710

Kentucky Historical Society
Corner of Lewis and Broadway
Frankfort, Ky. 40602
502-564-3016

Museum of the American Quilter's Society
215 Jefferson Street
PO Box 1540
Paducah, Ky. 42002-1540
270-442-8856

The Louisiana State Museum
751 Rue Chartres
New Orleans, La. 70116
504-568-6968

The Baltimore Museum of Art
Art Museum Drive
Baltimore, Md. 21218
410-396-6266

Maryland Historical Society
201 West Monument Street
Baltimore, Md. 21201-4674
410-685-3750

American Textile History Museum
491 Dutton Street
Lowell, Mass. 01854
978-441-0400

Historic Deerfield
Deerfield, Mass. 03421
413-774-5581

Museum of Fine Arts
Department of Textiles
465 Huntington Avenue
Boston, Mass. 02115
617-267-9300

New England Quilt Museum
18 Shattuck Street
Lowell, Mass. 01852
978- 452-4207

Old Sturbridge Village
1 Old Sturbridge Village Road
Sturbridge, Mass. 01566
508-347-3362

Dearborn Historical Museum
915 Brady Street
Dearborn, Mich. 48124
313-565-3000

Detroit Institute of Arts
5200 Woodard Avenue
Detroit, Mich. 48202
313-831-0360

The Edison Institute
Greenfield Village-Henry Ford Museum
20900 Oakwood Boulevard
Dearborn, Mich.
313-271-1620

Michigan State University Museum
Michigan State University
East Lansing, Mich. 48824
517-355-2370

Mississippi State Historical Museum
Mississippi Department of Archives and History
100 South State Street
Jackson, Miss. 39205
601-354-6222

The University Museum
The University of Mississippi
University, Miss. 38677
601-232-7073

Missouri Historical Society
Jefferson Memorial Building
Forest Park
St. Louis, Mo. 63112
314-361-1424

Powers Museum
1621 West Oak at Highway 71 Bypass
Carthage, Mo. 64836
417-358-2667

The St. Louis Art Museum
Forest Park
St. Louis, Mo. 63110
314-721-0067

Museum of the Rockies
Montana State University
Bozeman, Mont. 59717
406-994-2251

Joslyn Art Museum
2200 Dodge Street
Omaha, Nebr. 68102
402-342-3300

University of Nebraska –
Lincoln East Campus
International Quilt Study Center
207 HE Building, 35th and
Holdrege Streets
Lincoln, Nebr. 68583-0802
402-472-6342

Nevada Historical Society
1650 North Virginia Street
Reno, Nev. 89701
702-789-0190

New Hampshire Historical
Society
30 Park Street
Concord, N.H. 03301
603-225-3381

The Newark Museum
49 Washington Street
Newark, N.J. 07101
201-733-6600

Museum of International Folk
Art
Museum of New Mexico
706 Camino Lejo
Santa Fe, N.Mex. 87504
505-827-8350

Museum of American Folk Art
2 Lincoln Square
Columbus Ave. at 66th Street
New York, N.Y. 10023
212-595-9533

New York State Historical
Association
Fenimore House, Lake Road
Cooperstown, N.Y. 13326
607-547-1400

The Brooklyn Museum
200 Eastern Parkway
Brooklyn, N.Y. 11238
718-638-5000

The Metropolitan Museum of
Art
American Decorative Arts
Department
Fifth Avenue at 82nd Street
New York, N.Y. 10028
212-879-5500

The New York Historical Society
170 Central Park West
New York, N.Y. 10024
212-873-3400

Museum of Early Southern
Decorative Arts
924 South Main Street
Winston-Salem, N.C. 27108
919-722-6148

Cincinnati Art Museum
Art Museum Drive
Cincinnati, Ohio 45202
513-721-5204

Zoar Village State Memorial
Ohio Historical Society
Main Street
Zoar, Ohio 44697
216-874-3011

Pioneer Women Museum
701 Monument Road
Ponca City, Okla. 74604
405-765-6108

Latimer Quilt and Textile Center
2105 Wilson River Loop Road
Tillamook, Ore. 97141
503-842-8622

Ox Barn Museum
15038 2nd Street
Aurora, Ore. 97002
503-678-5754

Schminck Memorial Museum
128 South E Street
Lakeview, Ore. 97630
503-947-3134

The Heritage Center Museum
13 West King Street
Lancaster, Penn. 17603
717-299-6440

Philadelphia Museum of Art
Parkway at 26th Street
Philadelphia, Penn. 19101
215-787-5404

Rhode Island Historical Society
John Brown House
52 Power Street
Providence, R.I. 02906
401-331-8575

McKissick Museum
University of South Carolina
Columbia, S.C. 29208
803-777-7251

The Charleston Museum
360 Meeting Street
Charleston, S.C. 29403
803-722-2996

The Tennessee State Museum
505 Deaderick Street
Nashville, Tenn. 37219-5196
615-741-2692

Fort Worth Museum of Science
and History
1501 Montgomery Street
Fort Worth, Tex. 76107
817-732-1631

Texas Memorial Museum
University of Texas
2400 Trinity
Austin, Tex. 78705
512-471-3551

Territorial Statehouse
Fillmore, Utah 84631
801-743-5316

The Shelburne Museum
Shelburne Road, US Route 7
Shelburne, Vt. 05482
80985-3346

The Abby Aldrich Rockefeller
Folk Art Center
307 South England Street
Williamsburg, Va. 23187
804-229-1000

The Valentine Museum
1015 East Clay Street
Richmond, Va. 23219
804-649-0711

Washington State Historical
Society
315 North Stadium Way
Tacoma, Wash. 98403
206-593-2831

Yakima Valley Museum and
Historical Association
2105 Tierton Drive
Yakima, Wash. 98902
509-248-0747

Where to Buy
*As you get to know the antique
business and dealers in your area,
you will find people who are
knowledgeable in the field. These are
good people to ask about where to
find antique quilts for sale locally. The
following are a handful of good quilt
sources I can recommend.*

East Meets West
160 North La Brea Avenue
Los Angeles, Calif. 90036
323-931-0500

Julie Silber and Jean
Demeter/The Quilt Complex
PO Box 729
Albion, Calif. 95410
707-937-0739

Rebecca Proharenko
PO Box 863
Bellevue, Idaho 83313
208-788-2747

Shelly Zegart Quilts
300 Penruth Avenue
Louisville, Ky 40207
502-897-7566

Jill and Company
3744 Howard Avenue
Kensington, Md. 20895
301-946-7464

Stella Rubin Antiques
12300 Glen Road
Potomac, Md. 20854
301-948-4187

Cathy Smith
520 Moorings Circle
Arnold, Md. 21012
410-647-3503; 544-0050

David Wheatcroft
220 East Main Street
Westborough, Mass. 01581
508-366-1723

Laura Fisher/Antique Quilts &
Americana
1050 Second Avenue, Gallery 84
New York, N.Y. 10022
212-838-2596

Michele Fox American Antiques
The Old Meeting House
Route 9W and Closter Road
Palisades, N.Y. 10964
845-365-1540

Kelter Malce Antiques
74 Jane Street
New York, N.Y. 10014
212-675-7380

Judith and James Milne, Inc.
506 East 74th Street
New York, N.Y. 10021-3486
212-472-0107

Susan Parrish
390 Bleecker Street
New York, N.Y. 10014
212-645-5020

Woodard & Greenstein American
Antiques
506 East 74th Street, Fifth Floor
New York, N.Y. 10021-3486
212-988-2906

Oh Suzanna
16 South Broadway
Lebanon, Ohio 45036
513-932-8246

Chuck Auerbach
557 Letchworth Drive
Akron, Ohio 44303
330-867-0732

Mary and Joe Koval
182 Vine Street
Schellsburg, Penn. 15559
814-733-0092

Greg K. Kramer & Co.
27 West Freeman Street
Robesnia, Penn. 19551
610-693-3223

Rocky Road to Kansas
215 South Union Street
Alexandria, Va. 22314
703-683-0116

Acknowledgments

My deep appreciation goes to all those friends and colleagues who shared their quilts and photo images to make this project a success.

Many thanks to the following dealers who generously loaned their quilts: Mary and Joe Koval; Laura Fisher; Greg K.Kramer; Susan Parrish; Dixie Kaufman; Thomas K.Woodard and Blanche Greenstein; June Lambert; Julie Silber; Linda Reuther; Jill Rotter; David Wheatcroft; Judith and James Milne; Joel and Kate Kopp; and Michele Fox.

Collectors who kindly shared their quilts are: Eve Wilson; Polly Mello; Pat L. Nickols; Deborah Cooney; Toby and Oscar Fitzgerald; Theresa M. Michel; Kathy and Stan Scherer; John Wilmerding; Byron and Sara Dillow.

I appreciate the cooperation of the following institutions in allowing their images to be included: Doris Bowman of the Smithsonian Institution; Nancy Gibson of the DAR Museum; Old Sturbridge Village; Janey Fire of the Museum of American Folk Art; Cyril Nelson of Penguin Studio; and Pook and Pook, Inc.

I am particularly grateful to the editor, Melanie Hulse, whose knowledge of quilting was a great asset. I am similarly indebted to Deborah Cooney, whose understanding of quilts, as well as the English language, was a tremendous help.

Harriet Wise, who photographed many of the quilts for this book, demonstrated extraordinary patience and good humor, as well as skill at her craft.

Colleagues and friends were very generous in sharing ideas, experience, and information. Special thanks go to Joel and Kate Kopp, Bob Barone, and Leslie Kayne.

I greatly appreciate the staff of Mitchell Beazley for their unstinting support and encouragement, particularly Joseph Gonzalez. My thanks, too, for the work of Sara Hunt and Deborah DeFord.

My deepest thanks go to Lita Solis-Cohen, who planted the seed that allowed this book to take shape.